Marijuana
Recipes & Remedies

for Healthy Living

by Mary Jane Stawell

RONIN

Berkeley, California

www.roninpub.com

Note to Reader:

Information in this book is made available for informational purposes *only* under the authority of the First Amendment of the United States Constitution. The information presented is not meant to prescribe or to provide any medical advice. Readers should always consult with their personal physician before using marijuana as food or a remedy. Marijuana may be illegal in certain areas. The author and the publisher advocate no illegal activity of any kind, and make no implied or expressed warranties with respect to the information in this book. For legal advice, Readers should consult a licensed attorney.

Marijuana
Recipes & Remedies
for Healthy Living

by Mary Jane Stawell

**Marijuana Recipes & Remedies
for Healthy Living**

Copyright 2011: Beverly A. Potter

ISBN: 978-1-57951-133-3

Published by

Ronin Publishing, Inc.

PO Box 22900

Oakland, CA 94609

www.roninpub.com

All rights reserved. No part of this work may be reproduced or transmitted in any form by any means electronic or mechanical, including photocopying recording or translating into another language, or by any information storage or retrieval system, without written permission from the author or the publisher, except for inclusion of brief quotations in a review.

Library of Congress Card Number: 2011933025

Distributed to the book trade by PGW/Persesus

Printed in the United States

Mary Jane Stawell is a pseudonym.

Table of Contents

Table of Contents continued

Preface

FOLKS MAY GIGGLE when you speak about marijuana as food and a medical remedy since we tend to associate the "weed" with recreational uses rather than nutrition or medicine.

When eaten marijuana yields a different high that some describe as "deeper" or as having more of a body sensation. If your throat is feeling a little scratchy or a bit raw, you may not feel like smoking. Eating pot offers a valuable alternative when you are afraid that someone will smell it on your breath and clothes. Some people don't enjoy the taste of weed when smoked. If you are one of these people, you can see how eating it in a sweet food masks the taste but still gets you high.

But marijuana is more than a turn-on weed. It is a herb with nutritional and medicinal value. *Marijuana Recipes and Remedies* offers easy, delicious, nutritious recipes, including desserts of all kinds, breads, main courses, and elixirs. It teaches basic alchemical principles—such as how to use butter to extract herbal essence—so that you can experiment with your own creations. What fun!

Most cookbooks tell you how to cook "from scratch", which is great if you're a cook and you have enough time. But many us aren't "cooks"—yet we would like to incorporate marijuana herbals in our menu. *Marijuana Recipes and Remedies* is unique in that it includes how to use inexpensive, off-the-shelf, ready-made mixes you can find at the corner store to make some fabulous marijuana cuisine and how to make tinctures, poultices, and healing oils.

Marijuana As Healer

Soothing Herb

THE EUPHORIC EFFECTS OF MARIJUANA ORIGINATE from tetrahydrocannabinol—THC, the main active ingredient. THC is most concentrated in the marijuana flowers, often called "buds". Medicinal benefits include sedative, pain-soothing, and anti-inflammatory action, all of which stem from marijuana's palliative qualities. *Palliative* care is any form of medical treatment that concentrates on reducing the severity of symptoms, rather than curing the disease progression. Marijuana has strong palliative properties and can be used to prevent and relieve suffering and to improve the quality of life for people with serious, complex illness, such as cancer and Alzheimer's. Marijuana also has strong *analgesic* or pain-killing qualities stemming from its anti-inflammatory actions. An added benefit is that marijuana is not addictive as are stronger analgesics, like opioids.

Receptors

Marijuana, or *cannabis* as it is also called, contains over 60 oxygen-containing aromatic hydrocarbon compounds known as *cannabinoids*. Modern research into the therapeutic effects of the cannabinoids began in the 1960's with the identification of delta-9-tetrahydrocannabinol (THC) and cannabindiol (CBD) as the major psychoactive and non-psychoactive cannabinoids, respectively.

Anandamide

Some of THC's effects are useful in the world of medicine—like preventing nausea and blocking pain. Researchers have shown that the brain makes a chemical—*anandamide*—that attaches to the same nerve receptors as THC. When someone uses marijuana, these chemicals travel through the bloodstream and quickly attach to special places on the brain's nerve cells. These places are called *receptors*, because they receive information from other nerve cells and from chemicals. When a receptor receives information, it causes changes in the nerve cell. The chemical in marijuana that has a big impact on the brain is THC. Scientists recently discovered that some areas in the brain have a lot of THC receptors, while others have very few or none. These clues are helping researchers figure out exactly how THC works in the brain.

Marijuana research gained legitimacy with the discovery of these cannabinoid receptors in the 1990s. The cannabinoid receptor CB1 is widely expressed throughout the CNS, and seems to modulate psychoactive effects, motor control, memory processing, and pain. The endocannabinoids that are the natural ligands for the CB1 receptor are part of an endogenous physiologic system for regulating synaptic neurotransmission, analogous to that of opioids.

The distribution pattern of the CB1 receptors suggests that the typical effects of cannabinoids on cognition, memory, and motor performance could be mediated by their effects on cortical, hippocampal, basal ganglia, and cerebellar sites. These receptors are densely concentrated on output neurons in the outflow relay stations of the basal ganglia (substantial nigra and globus pallidus), where they are well-placed to affect movement control; receptors are sparser in most parts of the brain stem and spinal cord. Their presence in the nociceptive pathways of the brainstem and spinal cord suggests that they participate in a natural analgesic system.

Marijuana, the New Aspirin?

Marijuana is composed of more than 400 chemical components. A number of these components are found to provide therapeutic relief in alleviating chronic pain, seizure, depression and muscle spasms resulting from multiple sclerosis, but the primary psychoactive ingredient, THC, may produce some unwanted effects on human health, such as motor impairment.

To eliminate such unwanted effects, Physiologist Li Zhang and team are working to create a new kind of pain medication. Soon, people whose stomachs are too tender for aspirin or ibuprofen may be swallowing THC pills to get rid of headaches.

Zhang discovered that THC targets several parts of the nervous system, some of which are called inhibitory glycine receptors (GlyRs). These receptors, according to Zhang, help regulate "neuromotor activity, pain sensation, muscle relaxation and anxiety." He and his fellow researchers speculate that a synthetic THC could be made that targets just GlyRs to create a form of cannabis that works as a painkiller but doesn't get you high.

Zhang discovered a way to harness the painkilling powers of THC, while eliminating the high. What this means is that a special, non-hallucinatory version of THC—non-psychotropic cannabinoids—could become the new aspirin.

Health Benefits of Marijuana

1. **Treats Migraines**: More that 300,000 cases of migraines have been treated with marijuana.

2. **Slows Tumor Growth**: American Association for Cancer Research has found the marijuana works to slow down tumor growth in the lungs, breast, and brain.

3. **Relieves Symptoms of Chronic Diseases**: Marijuana can help treat the symptoms of chronic diseases like irritable bowel disease and Crohn's, because it can soothes nausea, abdominal pain and diarrhea.

4. <u>Prevents Alzheimer's</u>: The THC found in marijuana works to block deposits in the brain that are thought to cause Alzheimer's.

5. <u>Prevents Glaucoma</u> by lowering intraocular pressure in the eyes.

6. <u>Prevents Seizures:</u> It is a muscle relaxant with antispasmodic qualities.

7. <u>Benefits people with ADD & ADHD</u> without the negative side effects of Ritalin.

8. <u>Reduces multiple sclerosis symptoms</u> by stopping muscle spasms and protecting the nerves from damage.

9. <u>Helps relieve PMS pain</u> by soothing muscle cramps.

10. <u>Calms those with Tourette's & OCD</u> by slowing down the tics and obsessive neurological symptoms.

Pain Relief Points

There are four major links in the transmission chain where pain can be controlled.

1. **The initial injury site.** Pain can be managed directly at the site of injury with the use of a pain soothing ointments and compresses.

2. **The inflammatory response.** Minimizing the intercellular inflammatory response can reduce, even eliminate pain. The strategy is to eliminate foods that promote such inflammation from your diet and add anti-inflammatory foods to your diet.

3. **The message traveling along the nerves.** Interrupting the transmission of the message from the injury site to the brain is another pain management strategy. Hot chili peppers and cayenne pepper contain a remarkable substance called *capsaicin*, which is what gives peppers their kick. In the right dose, capsaicin blocks nerves' ability to transmit pain messages. It is the active ingredient in ointments used for arthritis, shingles, osteoarthritis and post-

mastectomy pain. A brief stinging sensation stimulates the nerves and shuts them down. They are thought to work by quickly depleting your nerves of a pain-signaling molecule called *substance P.*

4. The brain's perception of the pain. No matter how much irritation and injury there is an area of your body you will feel nothing until the pain messages reach the brain. The body makes natural pain killers called *enkephalins*, which means "in the head", and *endorphins*, which are natural morphine. Enkephalins are made in the adrenals the small glands that sit on top of the kidneys. Endorphins are made in the pituitary gland at the base of the brain.

Physical exercise stimulates release of these natural pain killers. A 6-mile run stimulates endorphin release roughly equivalent to 10 mil of morphine. The amino acid tryptophan, which produces serotonin in the brain soothes pain. High carb foods, like mashed potatoes with bud-butter, increase tryptophan concentration in the blood safely and reliably.

To Smoke or To Eat

DELIVERY SYSTEMS AVAILABLE TO MEDICAL MARIJUANA USERS include smoking, vaporization, tinctures, edibles, and topicals. Ingesting marijuana has many benefits over smoking it, including the elimination of dangerous chemicals entering the respiratory system. Eating marijuana leads to a markedly different experience from smoking. Eating marijuana-infused preparations usually leads to a longer, stronger, and much more physical high. Although eating is a perfectly viable way of absorbing marijuana into the bloodstream, higher amounts of the herb must be used in a cooking preparation in order to make the product effective. Consequently it is not always a cost-effective means to enjoy marijuana if the goal is to get high.

Edibles typically take 45-60 minutes to come on and the experience can last six to eight hours. One question frequently asked by patients new to using marijuana as medicine is the difference between smoking and ingesting edibles. When eaten marijuana is absorbed through the stomach, then processed by the liver before it reaches the brain. In the liver, THC is converted to 11-hydroxy-THC, a metabolite that is more psychoactive than ordinary THC. Because 11-hydroxy-THC is not produced when marijuana is smoked, eating and smoking produce different pharmacological effects. Some people regulate their medical conditions by eating small amounts of marijuana on a regular basis, sometimes just once or twice a day, like taking aspirin to soothe sore muscles. They barely feel any effect from the herb except for the relief of their symptoms. The major drawback of ingesting marijuana is that an effective dose is difficult to predict.

A popular method of eating marijuana is to cook with it. THC is fat-soluble, so to be released it must bind to either fatty acids or alcohol. Generally this is accomplished by heating oil, lard, or butter and marijuana to significant temperatures to release the THC to bind it to the lipid (fat) molecules. This "bud butter" can then be used in any recipe that requires butter or oil, from cookies to pancakes. The most popular means of cooking with marijuana is to add it to baked goods such as brownies.

The effect of eating food prepared with extracted marijuana will be more physical than heady and take an hour or more to reach your brain, before you feel it. However, once the hit arrives, it will be much stronger than for smoking an equivalent amount of pot, basically because you get 100% of it rather than losing quite a lot in the smoke and ash.

How Much to Eat

When eaten, cannabinoids are absorbed in a very different fashion from when marijuana is inhaled from a vaporizer or joint. When marijuana is inhaled, THC and cannabinoids in the pot enter the blood stream directly from the lungs and are quickly carried to the brain, causing a rapid onset of effects. As a result it is easy to know when you're "high" and have had enough. Not so, with marijuana foods. When eaten, effects can take as much as two hours to manifest. The marijuana-laden food goes to the stomach, not the lungs, where it must be digested and moved into the intestines for absorption into the bloodstream to be carried to the liver for processing, then to the cannabinoid receptors.

The problem here is that it is easy to misjudge the strength of the pot in the food. Thinking that nothing is happening, you can eat more before the effects of the first eating are experienced. By that time it is too late if you've eaten too much. With smoking or vaporizing, you simply pass when you've achieve your desired state, but with eating the THC and cannabinoids are in your intestines and surging around your bloodstream. In such overdosing, the effects can just keep coming on stronger and stronger to cause a bad experience. Short of induced vomiting or giving yourself an enema, neither of which may work, there's little you can do but ride it out.

Orally delivered marijuana requires four to ten times the amount of what you would smoke to achieve the same effect, which can present a problem in achieving the required or desired dose level in any consistent fashion.

Symptoms of Overdose

Eating too much marijuana can lead to a very unpleasant overdose experience. Some people report extreme gastrointestinal distress and severe spasms; others have hallucinations; some experience whirlies. Confusion, anxiety, paranoia, racing heart, even panic attacks, are common

You can never lose by eating too little because when you realize you have eaten too much, it is too late.

and may result in a trip to the emergency room. After effects of high-dose experiences, especially among those who are not regular users, can last 1-2 days.

Don't worry. There is no known case of anyone dying from an overdose of marijuana, but many folks who have eaten too much thought that they would die. There was a hilarious 911 tape of a police officer begging that an ambulance be dispatched because "we're dying". When asked what was going on, the cop explained that he busted a doper for possession, which he and his wife used to make brownies. It seems they ate *all* of them!!! He really did sound miserable as he repeatedly pleaded for an ambulance.

While eating too much marijuana is not life-threatening for healthy folks, overdosing can trigger a serious hypoglycemic reaction caused by a severe drop in blood sugar, which could pose a life-hazard to someone with undiagnosed diabetes, chronic hypoglycemia, and kidney or liver problems.

Bad experiences tends to happen when the power of marijuana is underestimated by folks who considers themselves to be a "very experienced" stoners. After all the high from smoking is pretty benign and easy to control because the effects are experienced almost immediately. So you can stop if the effects threaten to become too intense. Not so with eating.

Another common scenario is a few friends get together to bake some brownies and have a good time. Not knowing what to do, they often grind up a large quantity of pot or use a lot of bud-butter—way too much. They each sample a brownie. When little happens and being anxious to get the party going, they eat more. Bad idea! By the time that the effects begin to manifest it is too late. Consuming marijuana foods on an empty stomach is also chancy because the effects will be magnified.

No! No!s

Never sneak marijuana into an unsuspecting person's food or give someone tainted cookies or brownies without their knowledge. It may seem like a harmless prank. It isn't, especially if the person eats too much, like my friend Gene did. Without his knowing Gene's roommate cooked up a batch of cookies with some pretty potent weed. He offered Gene a scrumptious looking cookie loaded with chocolate chips, which Gene scarfed right down. Then the diabolical roommate set the plate stacked with cookies on the table next to Gene who was watching some engrossing TV show. You guessed it. Gene ate nearly all of the cookies. In about two hours—having no idea that he'd eaten pot, which he had never smoked—he was in a stupor and full panic attack and had to be taken to the hospital. Gene didn't think it was one bit funny.

Never eat any marijuana food before driving or operating machinery. Alcohol and prescription drugs can multiply the effects in unexpected ways. So be cautious about mixing alcohol with marijuana foods.

What To Do

Breathing slowly and deeply while focusing on your breaths, even counting to three or four between breaths helps many people to dispel anxiety. Drinking water seems to be universally helpful. Adding sugar to the water can also be helpful. Most importantly is to reassure yourself that there has never been any reported deaths from marijuana overdoes. You must ride it out.

It is a bad idea to go out into the world because you don't know how you will respond. Some people report losing coordination and falling, sometimes being unable to speak. This behavior can trigger such alarm other people, especially if you insist that you're dying, that you might be hauled off to the hospital—which would really be a drag. The best precaution is to be smart. Don't eat too much! And stay put.

Titration

Some people can tolerate much more marijuana food than others! Body weight and metabolism matters. Make sure to titrate—eat a little and wait about an hour to check the effects. Then eat a little more. Remember, marijuana food could take anywhere from 20 minutes to 2 hours to fully kick in!

Titration is a process used to determine how much of a medication to take by gradually adjusting the dose until the desired effect is achieved. Eat a small portion of the marijuana-laced food and then wait an hour to evaluate the effects. Then, if you choose, eat another small portion and wait another half hour or so. Through this process you can decide how much to eat. The problem here is that marijuana potency varies from plant to plant, so that every batch of cookies or brownies will have a different potency.

Foods That Fight Pain

BACK IN THE SIXTIES TINY TIM TOLD US that we are what we eat, which came as a revelation. Whoa, who knew?! Food influences our bodies and our health? Wow!!! Of course, you know if you eat a lot of sweets and fats you'll develop a spare tire. Foods you eat have a greater impact on your than being the source of your energy and fat storage. Many very popular foods, like chocolate, milk, hamburgers and fries, are like a subtle form of poison ivy in sensitive people—they trigger inflammation pain.

When you cut your finger, the injured area turns red, gets warm, swells, and gets sores. This reaction is called *inflammation*. Your body increases blood flow to the injury, bringing in healing nutrients and white blood cells to swallow up the germs. Inflammation contributes to headaches, digestive problems, menstrual cramps, psoriasis, eczema, arthritis, as well as cancer and other conditions.

Fats and Inflammation

Inflammation is controlled by a natural compound, called *prostaglandins* and their chemical relatives, all of which are made from traces of fat that have been stored inside the cells. Fats that you eat determine which of the prostaglandins will be produced. Some fats fan the flames of inflammation while others cool them down. Diets rich in meats, dairy products, shortenings and cooking oils, like corn oil or cotton seed oil pack unfriendly inflammatory fats into the cell membranes surrounding the cells, causing even more pain.

Two fats from plants act like anti-inflammatory medicines, without the side effects of drugs. Alpha-linolenic acid, or ALA, is found in many common foods, including walnuts, soy products, wheat germ, canola oil and concentrated in flax seed and flax seed oil, and Gamma-linolenic acid, or GLA, is rarer and found in a few seed oils and hemp oil. ALA and GLA pack the cells with helpful anti-inflammatory compounds. These natural fats can be used to fight inflammation to reduce joint swelling, tenderness and morning stiffness. By comparison, olive oil, corn oil sunflower oil, safflower oil, lard, butter and other common fats and oils do not have anti-inflammatory action. It can take several weeks for oils to work, even up to six months. ALA is also found in green leafy vegetables, beans, and other legumes and fruits.

> *Let food be thy medicine and medicine be thy food.*
>
> —Hippocrates

Natural Oils with ALA and GLA Content

ALA Content		GLA Content	
Canola oil	11%	Black currant oil	17-18%
Flaxseed oil	53-62%	Borage oil	24%
Linseed oil	53%	Evening Primrose oil	8-10%
Soybean oil	7%	Hemp oil	19%
Walnut oil	10%	Wheat-germ oil	7%

If you suffer pain caused by inflammation, including digestive problems, menstrual cramps, psoriasis, eczema, arthritis, as well as cancer and other conditions, you would probably benefit from avoiding common fats, including butter. The problem is that many medical marijuana recipes call for bud-butter, which probably increases inflammation. You can avoid this problem by substituting one of the oils with ALA or GLA, such an canola oil in preparing bud-oil you can use in cooking.

Inflammatory Foods

If you have pain caused by inflammation you can dramatically reduce your pain by avoiding pro-inflammatory foods. Steer clear of sodas and sugary juice drinks because they seem to increase pain–causing it to come on sooner and more intensely. Any drink with high fructose corn syrup should also be avoided. Processed sugars and other high-glycemic starches increase inflammation, just as they raise blood sugar, Watch for sugar content in salad dressings. Unfortunately many marijuana edibles available in the clubs are made from just these ingredients!

Multi-Symptom Triggers

Foods identified as triggers for migraines, arthritis, irritable bowel syndrome, Crohn's disease, and fibromyalgia.

Dairy products[1]	Wheat	Citrus Fruits
Corn, Cornstarch	Caffeine	Meat[2]
Nuts	Tomatoes	Eggs

[1]Includes skim, whole cow's milk, goat's milk, cheese, yogurt.
[2]Includes beef, pork, chicken, turkey, fish

In headaches, joint pain and digestive pain the key is not so much as adding new foods than in finding out what food cause your pain and avoiding them, while eating foods that almost never cause symptoms.

Add Pain-Soothing Foods to Your Diet

Foods that improve blood flow aid in reducing angina, back pain and leg pains. Foods that relieve inflammation help your joints to cool down. Rice and pepper oil can soothe the digestive track. Ginger can prevent migraines. Coffee sometimes cures them. Natural plant oils can reduce arthritis pain. Cranberry juice fights the pain of bladder infections.

Ginger

Ginger is a wonderful herb that blocks inflammation in musculoskeletal disorders. It is good for soothing headaches and nausea. It has been widely used for centuries as arthritis treatment. Ginger works by blocking histamines and inhibiting prostaglandins, which are the chemicals that play a role in inflammation. Other spices that work in similar way are clove oil, garlic, turmeric, and cumin. Any of these medicinal herbs can be combined with marijuana to yield individualized portions for relief from your condition.

The amount of ginger is ½ to 1 teaspoon of powdered ginger each day. It tends to take 4 to 12 weeks for the benefits to appear. There are not adverse effects reported.

Pain-Safe Foods

Pain-safe foods tend to not encourage inflammation. Anti-inflammatory foods include brown rice, cooked or died fruits, cherries, cranberries, pears, prunes, but not citrus fruits or apples, bananas, peaches or tomatoes. Other anti-inflammatory foods include cooked green, yellow or orange vegetables, artichokes, asparagus, broccoli, chard, collards, lettuce, spinach, string beans, summer or winter squash, sweet potatoes, tapioca, and plain or carbonated water

Foods affect joints in much the same way as it does headaches. Corn is a common trigger for arthritis and includes cornstarch. Some people have had dramatic improvement when corn was removed from their diets. Rheumatoid arthritis is among the aggravating of joint problems. It causes pain and stiffness and deforms joints. Some people believe that it is an auto-immune disease where the white blood cells attack the tissues that line your joints. By changing the foods you eat you can often reduce pain. Swelling and stiffness in joints can improve and even go away. Some people have suffered for years with arthritis never realizing that simple diet changes can be a big help.

Certain foods are frequent offenders while other are almost always safe. Red wine and chocolate are among the worst migraine triggers but not much of a problem in arthritis. Corn and wheat are often indicated in arthritis and less often in migraines. Milk products are high on the list of offenders, includes milk chocolate so medical marijuana patients need to pay attention to the edibles because so often they are made of sugar and chocolate, both of which are among the food offenders in many cases causing pain.

Digestive Problems, Ulcers, Heart Burn, Irritable Bowel Syndrome

It can help to take advantage of food that calm down the digestive track and avoid those that send it into spasms. Peppermint oil and ginger are particularly good for soothing digestive pains. Rice is nutritional and well-tolerated; brown rice is best. Oat products are rich in solvable fiber—plant roughage that dissolves in water, whereas insolvable fiber is found in wheat and other grains.

Solvable fiber also reduces cholesterol levels and helps digestions. Vegetables are rich in solvable fiber and are well-tolerated when well-cooked without fat. Beans, peas, and lentils are loaded with solvable fiber. There is no fiber at all in refined sugar and you are better off avoiding it completely. However, again, the problem is that many marijuana edibles sold in the clubs are cookies, candies and brownies—all packed with inflammation promoting sugar.

Foods That Can Trigger Irritable Bowel Syndrome

Fatty foods, hamburger, greasy fries, potato chips, drum stick, are a key contributor to irritable bowel syndrome. Dairy products, especially the milk sugar called *lactose* can irritate the bowels. Eggs, wheat, corn, barley and rice can be a problem. Coffee and tea. Raw fruit, including citrus, apples, grapes, cantaloupe, bananas, and raw vegetables, including broccoli, cauliflower, brussels sprouts, cabbage, tomatoes, spinach, and peppers.

Most people experience dramatic improvement after eliminating fatty and other problem foods and emphasizing natural high-fiber foods in their diets. Additionally peppermint oil has been used since the 1700's to soothe digestive aliments. The active ingredient is menthol which relaxes the muscles of the digestive tract. You might experiment with adding peppermint oil with bud-oil which has muscle soothing qualities.

Prostrate Cancer

Prostrate cancer has been consistently linked with the consumption of animal products like milk, meat, eggs, cheese, cream and butter. High fat and low fiber diets increase testosterone in the man's body which fuels the growth of prostrate cells, causing benign prostrate enlargement and encourages the growth of cancer cells. Prostrate cancer is less common in people who consume more vegetables, fruits and soybean products. First, they are low in fat and rich in fiber. And they also tend to reduce testosterone levels. Fiber soaks up testosterone in the intestines and carries it away. Vegetables, beans and grains keep the body's removal system working, but fish, chicken, eggs and animal products have no fiber to remove the excess testosterone so it in absorbed in the intestines and becomes active again.

Men who eat plenty of strawberries and tomatoes have less risk of prostrate cancer because of the red pigment, *lycopene*. Tomatoes are rich in lycopene. Cooked tomatoes are even more protective than are the raw ones. Men who eat ten or more servings a week of tomato juice, spaghetti, raw tomatoes and tomato paste foods, even pizza, have up to 45% less risk of getting prostrate cancer. Lyocopene is also found in watermelon, pink grapefruit and guavas.

Breast Cancer

Like prostrated cancer there is a relationship between high fat and low fiber diets and breast cancer versus the opposite, which has a lower rate of breast cancer. Animal fats appear to be even a bigger problem in promoting breast cancer than vegetable oils.

What Is Glycemic Index?

The Glycemic Index (GI) is a numerical scale used to indicate how fast and how high a particular food can raise our blood glucose (blood sugar) level. A food with a low GI will typically prompt a moderate rise in blood glucose, while a food with a high GI may cause our blood glucose level to increase above the optimal level.

An awareness of foods' Glycemic Index can help you control your blood sugar levels, and by doing so, may help you prevent heart disease, improve cholesterol levels, prevent insulin resistance and type-2 diabetes, prevent certain cancers, and achieve or maintain a healthy weight. A substantial amount of research suggests a low GI diet provides these significant health benefits. So, it's worth taking a look at the basic principles of a low GI way of eating.

A healthy eating plan that enables you to maintain a low to moderate Glycemic Index has great potential importance in treating and preventing chronic disease.

Persons with diabetes, in particular, can reap significant benefits from a low to moderate GI way of eating. In persons with diabetes, an uncontrolled glucose level—which means blood glucose levels are often too high—can lead to severe health complications including heart disease, blindness, kidney failure and limb amputations.

Have you ever noticed that you feel lethargic after eating foods that stimulate a large insulin response, such as donuts or candy? This often happens because too much insulin is produced in response to such foods, and this excess insulin causes blood sugar levels to drop below normal, resulting in low blood sugar (hypoglycemia) and fatigue.

When this happens, people who are unaware that the high sugar food they just ate is the reason for their sudden drop in energy reach for another sweet or high carbohydrate food, which starts the cycle all over again. When your blood sugar is bouncing from too high to too low repeatedly throughout the day, you certainly don't feel your best. On the other hand, when your food choices help you maintain consistent normal blood sugar levels, you feel great and have the energy you need to enjoy long, active days.

For example, for breakfast, you might want to have oatmeal. Choose thick, dehulled oat flakes to make your oatmeal (these have a lower GI than rolled oats or one-minute oats), then eat grapefruit (one of the lower GI fruits) with your oatmeal rather than a banana (a fruit with a higher GI), and toss a few nuts or seeds over the oatmeal (nuts and seeds tend to have extremely low GIs). Top off your oatmeal with a little bud-milk and/or bud-butter, which adds a pleasant earthy taste. Finally, sprinkle a little cinnamon over your oatmeal. Recent studies have found that compounds in cinnamon can stimulate our cells' insulin receptors, increasing the cells' ability to absorb and use glucose. In this way, you can reduce the GI of your oatmeal and enjoy a nourishing breakfast that will provide you with plenty of energy all morning.

Cooking Basics

U SING INFUSED OILS AND BUTTERS are the most common ways to cook with marijuana. When you've mastered the art of a great bud-butter or bud-oil, you can cook marijuana into virtually anything calling for these ingredients. They are simply substituted in dishes that would call for regular oil or butter. Delicious! You can add marijuana to any food that contains animal or vegetable fats, such as cakes, biscuits, stews or drinks such as milk shakes, drinking chocolate or yoghurt.

Cannabinoids are chemicals in marijuana. Interestingly, they are also found in our nervous and immune systems. The body binds naturally produced cannabinoids with nervous-system receptors—cannabinoid receptors called CB1 and CB2—to regulate mood, appetite, pain sensation, inflammation response and memory. When THC from marijuana is consumed in food, it binds to the cannabinoid receptors in the same way that the naturally occurring cannabinoids do, which is how marijuana helps to soothe pain and enliven mood. By the way, opiates in opium and heroin relieve pain through the same process—the opiates bind with opiate receptors, which then act to reduce pain.

Indica v. Sativas

Marijuana comes in two general varieties—*Cannabis Indica* and *Cannabis Sativa*. Indica is a shorter plant with broader leaves and has less of a euphoric high. Having a higher level of cannabinoids than Sativas, Indica yields a sedated body-type effect and is generally chosen for its medicinal properties—the anti-epileptic, anti-inflammatory and stimulant properties. Indica effects the body, providing feelings of relaxation, calm and serenity. Generally, folks pick an Indica strain for relief of pain and as a sleep aid. Indicas are sedatives/relaxants and effective for soothing anxiety, chronic pain, insomnia, muscle spasms and tremors.

Sativas have a higher level of THC than Indicas, which results in a psychoactive and energetic mind-high. Sativa strains may cause feelings of alertness and optimism. Due to its high THC content, Sativa's effects are mostly cerebral, giving feelings of well-being. It is a good choice for a daytime high, which is characterized as energetic and uplifting. Sativa strains are more of a stimulant, and are effective in appetite stimulation, relieving depression, migraines, chronic pain and nausea.

There are also hybrids of Sativa plus Indica. Hybrids and cross-breeds of Indica and Sativa strains produce varieties that carry some characteristics of each parent. For example, adding Sativa to Indica strains adds mental clarity and decreases sedation effects. Adding Indica to Sativa strains can decrease or even eliminate the Sativa tendency to stimulate anxiety.

A rough rule of thumb is to select Indica dominant strains for cramping and muscle spasticity and Sativa dominant strains for mental pick up.

Some marijuana food recipes use finely ground marijuana but this makes for a rather crunchy experience that some likened to a cow chewing its cud. More importantly, however, is that it is inefficient because the THC and other cannabinoids remain bound up in the plant during the digestion process and are excreted along with the roughage, so most of the pot is wasted. THC is easily released by smoking but THC is not readily digested. It must be extracted into a form that the body can metabolize.

Because THC is insoluble in water, it must be extracted into fat, oil or alcohol in order to bind with the cannabinoid receptors. THC is delicate and must be slowly combined with butter or oil over fairly low heat so that it does not break down and vaporize.

Bud-oil and bud-butter must be cooked for a long period of time to slowly absorb the cannabinoids into the fat molecules to be a vehicle for the THC. These fats also aid absorption into the body. When digested, these cannabinoid-infused fat molecules bind with our buddies, the cannabinoid receptors CB1 and CB2 to distribute the infused THC.

Remember fat or alcohol is needed to extract the THC from the marijuana plant. Whole milk contains 8 grams of fat for every 8 ounces, 2% milk contains 5 grams of fat, 1% contains 2.5 grams of fat, and skim milk contains no fat. Cocoa is not the same as chocolate. Hot cocoa is made from cocoa powder and lacks the fat of cocoa butter so it is not good for THC extraction. By comparison, hot chocolate is made from chocolate bars melted into cream.

The basic principle in cooking with marijuana is that the THC and other cannabinoids must be extracted from the plant. Then the extraction is used in cooking. Because THC is soluble in oil and alcohol these can be used to extract it from the leaf and bud. Cooking ground up marijuana in butter or various oils releases the plant's essence, which flows into the oil.

Whether to use butter or which oil depends. Butter, being a saturated fat, can pose health issues. Olive oil is considered to be among the healthiest oils due to its high content of monounsaturated fatty acids and its high content of antioxidative substances. Olive oil has anti-inflammatory properties. Most people do quite well with it since it does not upset the critical omega 6 to omega 3 ratio and most of the fatty acids in olive oil are actually an omega-9 oil, which is monounsaturated. Some people don't like the taste of olive oil. You can experiment with other anti-inflammatory oils, which include coconut oil and almond oil.

Bud-Butter

Bud-butter, which is THC extracted into butter, is the basic marijuana cooking ingredient. Bud-butter can be substituted for the called for butter or oil in almost any recipe. If you fry breakfast eggs in butter, try using a teaspoon of bud-butter as your frying medium.

Half-Pound of Bud-Butter

People on anti-inflammatory diets to reduce pain, should use canola oil for extraction, because butter is an inflammatory food that can trigger migraines and arthritis flair ups in sensitive people.

Potency

When using the best Grade A marijuana, use a ratio of 1 ounce of marijuana to 16-20 ounces of bud-butter. This will yield 100-125 teaspoons of very potent extract. When using Grade B marijuana, use a ratio of one ounce of marijuana to 8 ounces of butter to yield 50 teaspoons of extract. With Grade C marijuana you'll need to use a high marijuana-to-butter ratio, such as one ounce of marijuana to 4 ounces of butter. With seeds and stems, use an especially high ratio of marijuana to butter.

Water Bath Extraction

Bring 2-3 quarts of water to boil in a large pot, then reduce the heat to a low simmer. Add ground up marijuana and stir with wooden spoon. Cover and gently simmer on low for two hours. Stir occasionally. Be sure that you do not boil the mixture. Add butter and stir until the butter is completely melted. Cover and continue to gently simmer for two more hours, stirring frequently.

Pour the buttery mixture through the strainer into a bowl. Heat a small kettle of water to boiling and slowly pour the boiling water through the strainer while shaking it to remove all of the liquid butter from the marijuana mash. Press the mash in the strainer to squeeze out all of the liquid, then discard the marijuana mash.

Cover the bowl with liquid buttery mixture and set aside to cool. When room temperature put into the refrigerator overnight. The mixture will separate into two to three layers when cold. Using a knife, pry up the hardened butter and break into pieces. A second creamy, semisolid layer under the hardened butter should be removed carefully with a spoon. Be careful to not stir it into the liquid below it, which is mostly water with dissolved plant matter and semi-emulsified butter particles.

Mix the hardened butter with the creamy mix from the second layer into a paste, which is ready for cooking. Some people use the watery liquid from the third layer in sauces and soups and to cook noodles or rice.

Alcohol Bath Extraction

Extracting with alcohol bath is more efficient than with the water bath because alcohol is a more effective solvent. Whereas THC does not dissolve in water, in an alcohol bath the THC molecules are liberated and absorbed by the alcohol. The alcohol is then evaporated away as the active THC is absorbed by the butter. The alcohol bath produces a more

Always use double boiler with alcohol.

potent butter extract. Any high-proof alcohol can be used. Rum and vodka are particularly popular.

For alcohol bath extraction always use a double boiler on a hot plate or electric stove. Heating alcohol with gas flame is dangerous and should be avoided to prevent explosion and fire. Good ventilation is important because as the alcohol heats it produces explosive fumes.

Heat the water in the bottom of the double boiler

Improvised double boiler

to a low simmer. Add crushed marijuana and one cup of alcohol for each ounce of marijuana to the top of the boiler. When the alcohol warms, add 8 ounces—two sticks—of butter for each ounce of marijuana. Cover and cook for several hours. Make sure to keep enough water in the bottom of the boiler to keep the mixture at a low simmer. Toward the end of cooking, allow the alcohol to evaporate. Pour the green liquid and marijuana through a strainer into a bowl. Press the marijuana mash to drain off the emerald green liquid.

Storing Bud-Butter

It is best to make only as much bud-butter as you need for a particular recipe because it can get stale and go rancid. However, it is convenient to have prepared bud-butter on hand, especially if you are cooking for only one or two. One great method is to freeze it in ice cube trays. Each cube will be approximately ¼ cup of bud-butter. When a recipe calls for ½ cup of butter, you simply pop out two cubes and drop into your recipe.

How to Make Bud Cooking Oil

Ingredients:

    48 oz bottle canola cooking oil

    Large-sized cooking pot

    1 oz of marijuana buds

    Metal strainer

POUR CANOLA OIL into the cooking pot. Heat on medium until hot. Do not allow to boil. Crumble marijuana into small bits and add to hot oil. Stir oil herb mixture every ten minutes for two hours. If the mixture starts to boil remove the from heat and let cool and turn burner heat down.

Recipes

Breakfasts

Zucchini Bread

Ingredients:

    4 eggs

    1 1/2 cups bud-butter,

    3 cups sugar

    4 cups zucchini, shredded

    2 1/2 tsp vanilla extract   Makes 2 loaves

    4 cups all purpose flour

    1/2 tbsp baking soda

    1/2 tbsp salt

    1 cup walnuts, chopped

    Basil sprig

PRE-HEAT OVEN TO 325° F. Combine eggs, bud-butter, sugar, and zucchini in a bowl. In a second bowl combine vanilla, flour, baking soda, salt and walnuts. Add wet ingredients to dry ingredients and stir until incorporated. Divide into 2 oiled loaf pans and bake for approximately one hour. Test with toothpick, which should come out clean when done. Slice and garnish with basil.

Pancakes

Ingredients:

   1/4 cup flour

   2 tbsp baking powder

   2 tsp sugar

   1/2 tsp salt

   Pinch of cinnamon

   2 tbsp of bud-oil

   1/2 cup water

   3/4 cup bud-milk

PRE-HEAT GRIDDLE OVER MEDIUM HIGH FLAME while making the pancake batter. Griddle is ready when drops of water sizzle, then evaporate. Combine dry ingredients in a large bowl and mix thoroughly. Combine wet ingredients in a second bowl and mix well. Pour the wet mixture into the dry and mix. The batter should be somewhat lumpy, which makes the pancakes light and fluffy. Pour batter on to slightly oils griddle. Flip the pancakes when the surface bubbles up. Serve with bud-butter and maple syrup.

Quickie Aunt Jemima Bud-Milk Pancakes

AUNT JEMIMA BRAND SELLS A SMALL, PANCAKES for two size packet very inexpensively, often available in convenience type stores that carry a limited line of groceries, like 7-11 and Walgreen's. It great for making bud-milk pancakes. Just pour the powdered mix in a bowl. Substitute bud-milk for water and mix, leaving lumpy. Cook on hot griddle. Serve with bud-butter and maple syrup. Makes eight to ten 4-inch pancakes.

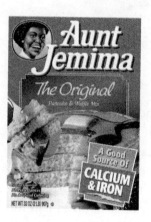

Marijuana Banana Bread

Ingredients: Makes 2 loaves

    1/2 cup bud-butter

    2 eggs

    1 tsp lemon juice

    3 tsp baking powder

    1 cup sugar

    1 cup bananas, mashed

    2 cups flour, sifted

    1/2 tsp salt

    1 cup nuts, chopped

PRE-HEAT OVEN 375° F. Mix bud-butter and sugar together in a large mixing bowl. Beat the eggs and add to the mixture. In separate bowl, mash bananas, mix in the lemon juice, then add to egg and sugar mixture. Sift the flour, salt, and baking powder together then add to the banana mixture. Mix in chopped nuts. Bake in bread pan for 1 hour and 15 minutes. Remove banana bread from oven, put a towel over it and set aside until cool. Slice and serve.

Quickie Oatmeal Breakfast

INSTANT OATMEAL CEREAL IS VERY NUTRITIOUS. It is low in saturated fat, very low in cholesterol, and a good source of vitamin A, vitamin E (alpha trocopherol), thiamin, riboflavin, niacin and Vitamin B-12, and a very good source of Vitamin B-6, folate, calcium, iron and manganese. However, some commercial products may have a high sugar content.

Ingredients: Serves 1

    Packet of instant oatmeal mix

    1/2 cup bud-milk

    1 tsp bud-butter

    Strawberries, blueberries optional

Empty oatmeal mix into small bowl, add bud-milk or water and microwave for 1-2 minutes. Garnish with bud-milk or bud-butter. Best to use bud-milk or bud-butter, but not both until your body is acclimatized to marijuana cooking.

Hemp Milk

HEMP MILK CONTAINS 33 PERCENT PROTEIN and offers well-balanced essential fatty acids, including the anti-inflammatory GLA, that our bodies require and don't make themselves. The key for making quick and easy hemp milk is to buy shelled hemp seeds. Check the dates on the seeds to make sure that they are fresh. Store hemp seeds in a dark place because sunlight will destroy the oils' benefits and make the seeds rancid.

Ingredients:

    1/4 cup shelled hemp seeds

    1 cup water

    Flavorings: vanilla, maple syrup or honey

Place seeds into a blender and add small amount of water 1 inch above the seeds. Turn blender on at multiple speeds and agitate seeds so they become a thick hemp cream. Then add either vanilla, maple syrup or honey or only a ripe banana and serve as a thick drink or add water at a ratio of 4.75 water to 1 part seed for a lighter hemp milk.

Raw Almond Bud-Butter

Ingredients: Makes a 10-oz jar.

2 cups almonds, shelled

3 tsp almond or coconut oil

¼ cup marijuana, ground

Pinch of salt

PLACE ALMONDS IN A FOOD PROCESSOR or high-speed blender and process until they become fine crumbs. Slowly add in salt and oil and process until it becomes a smooth past, adding more oil to reach the desired texture. Transfer to a jar and refrigerated.

Main Courses

Marijuana Chili

Ingredients:

   2 lbs. pinto beans

   1 lb. bacon, cut into two inch sections

   2 cups red wine

   4 tbsp chili powder

   1/2 garlic clove

   1 cup marijuana, chopped

   1/2 cup mushrooms

SOAK BEANS OVERNIGHT IN WATER. In a large pot, pour boiling water over beans and simmer for at least an hour, adding more water to keep beans covered. Cook bacon in a large frying pan. When about half cooked, pour off about half of the bacon lard. Add the chopped marijuana to the cooking bacon and sauté for 15 minutes. Do not burn. Add marijuana-bacon mix and all other ingredients to the simmering beans and continue to simmer for another three hours. Salt to your own taste. Serve with parsley garnish.

Hemp Sushi Salad

Ingredients

  2 tbsp hemp seed oil

  1/2 cup shelled hemp seed

  2 cups rice, cooked

  1 cucumber, thinly sliced

  2 tbsp vinegar

  1 tbsp soy sauce

  2 sheets toasted nori, cut into small pieces

  1 cup green onion, finely diced

  1/4 cup pickled ginger, cut into small strips

  2 tbsp hot pepper sesame oil (optional)

  1 tbsp ginger, fresh grated (optional)

COMBINE AND MIX WELL OILS, VINEGAR, soy sauce, and ginger. To create the salad, make the first layer rice. Layer the cucumber slices on top of that. Pour dressing over cucumbers and rice. Sprinkle shelled hemp seeds on top. Garnish with ginger strips first, then onion, then strips of nori.

Marijuana Meat Balls

Ingredients: Serves 4

1 lb. hamburger, lean

1/4 cup onions, chopped

1 can cream of mushroom soup

1/4 cup bread crumbs

3 tbsp marijuana, finely ground

3 tbsp relish

PUT HAMBURGER into large bowl. Mix in onions, crumbs, marijuana and relish. Shape into golf ball-size meatballs. Brown in frying pan and drain. Place meatballs in a casserole bowl.
Mix soup with 1/2 cup water, and pour over meatballs. Cover and bake in 350° F oven for about 30 minutes.

Garlic Basil Marijuana Mashed Potatoes

Ingredients:

    3-4 large russet potatoes, cubed

    6 large garlic cloves, chopped

    3 tsp olive oil

    3 tbsp basil, finely chopped

    1 tbsp black pepper

    1 tsp salt

    1/4 pint cream

    4-6 oz ricotta cheese

    1/4 cup bud-butter

MIX CHOPPED GARLIC INTO OLIVE OIL AND SAUTÉ in small frying pan until brown. Boil the cubed potatoes in salted water until fork tender, drain, and mash lightly. Add

butter to potatoes and continue to mash. Add pepper, salt, cream, and cheese and mash until smooth. Mix in garlic and whip until smooth. Leave skins on the potatoes for extra nutrition and a home-style taste. Garnish with crumbled bacon. You can crumble bacon into your mashed potatoes for an extra crunch; or for a home-style taste, leave the skin on the potatoes.

Quickie Mashed Potatoes

Ingredients:

Pouch of instant mash potato mix

2 1/2 cups water

1/4 cup bud-butter

1/2 cup cold milk*

1/2 cup cold bud-milk

1/4 cup parsley, chopped

Boil WATER and add bud-butter. Remove from heat and add milk and bud-milk and stir while adding pouch of potatoes. Let stand for 1-2 minutes.
Garnish with chopped parsley and glob of bud-butter. *Begin with half regular milk and half bud-milk. Titrate this recipe to determine how much bud-milk to use.

Twice-Baked Baked Potatoes

Ingredients: Serves 2-4

    1-2 12-ounce Idaho potatoes

    2-4 tbsp bud-butter

    1/8 tsp salt

    Ground pepper to taste

    Green onion, sliced crosswise

    2 oz graded cheddar cheese

    1/2 tsp cayenne pepper

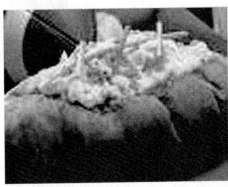

PREHEAT OVEN TO 400° F. Poke holes in potatoes with fork and for 50 minutes. Remove potatoes and let cool to touch. Slice potatoes in half length-wise. Scoop out potato flesh, leaving behind about 1/4 inch of skin and flesh. Mash the scooped flesh with the bud-butter, salt, pepper, and onion. Stuff the mixture back into the skins and top with grated cheese. Return potato to the oven and bake until cheese is melted. Garnish with cayenne pepper.

Roasted Garlic Chicken
with Angel Hair Pasta

Ingredients: Serves 4

16 oz angel hair pasta

2 garlic heads

2 cups vinegar

4 oz jar of pimentos

4 chicken breasts

Bud-oil

Salt

PREHEAT OVEN TO 400° F. Cook pasta according to package directions. Remove outer skin of garlic while leaving the head intact. Cut off the top end of the head of garlic, about ¼—½ inch, so that the inner cloves are exposed. Drizzle the top of the garlic with bud-oil and a little salt, then wrap tightly in aluminum foil, place in a baking pan and roast for approximately 30 minutes, or until very fragrant and soft.

Season chicken breasts with salt and pepper. Brown chicken on both sides in large skillet over high heat. When fully cooked, remove from skillet and set aside. Add vinegar and pimentos with juice to the skillet in which chicken was cooked. Squeeze the roasted garlic out of the cloves into the pan and smash with a fork. Simmer mixture until the volume has reduced by about ¼. Add chicken into mixture in skillet and simmer until sauce has thickened. Serve chicken and sauce over pasta.

Meatloaf Marijuana

Ingredients:

    1/4 oz marijuana, ground

    1 lb ground beef, lean

    1 large egg

    1/2 package saltines, crushed

    1 packet Lipton's Tomato Cup-A-Soup

    1/2 cup green pepper, chopped

    1/2 cup onion, chopped

    1 loaf pan

    Ketchup (optional)

PREHEAT OVEN TO 350° F. In a large bowl, combine ground beef, onion, and green pepper and mix with hands.

Kneed in saltines, soup, and marijuana. Roll the beef mix into a ball and press a hole into it and drop in the egg. Kneed the beef and egg until mixed thoroughly. Spread into loaf pan and garnish top with ketchup. Bake in oven for 30 minutes.

Quick Tuna & Olive Pasta

Ingredients: Serves 4

2 - 6 oz cans tuna in olive oil

½ cup pitted olives, sliced

1 ½ cups cannelloni beans

2 tsp lemon juice

Half medium lemon

2 tbsp parsley, finely chopped

2 tbsp celery leaves, finely chopped

½ tsp crushed red pepper flakes

1/4 cup bud-oil

½ lb spaghetti

Salt to taste

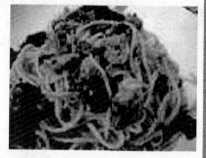

IN A LARGE BOWL, combine tuna with its oil, sliced olives, beans, lemon juice, lemon zest, parsley, celery leaves, and red pepper flakes. Add half the bud-oil and lightly toss until well combined. Cook pasta in a large pot of boiling salted water, uncovered, until al dente. Drain and return to the pot. Add the tuna mixture to the pot and toss well. Add remaining bud-oil and lightly toss until pasta is well coated. Warm until just heated through. Season with salt to taste. Garnish with additional chopped fresh parsley, and drizzle with virgin olive oil. Serve immediately.

Marijuana Stir Fry

Ingredients:

    1 red pepper

    1 green pepper

    1 yellow pepper

    1/2 onion, chopped

    4 tbsp bud-butter

    Chicken, steak or shrimp, cut into strips or cubes

    Rice, steamed

CUT PEPPERS INTO LONG STRIPS about 1/2 to 3/4 inches wide put into a skillet with the bud-butter. Add the onions and meat strips or cubes. Sauté until meat starts to brown and veggies are cooked. Serve over rice.

Cream of Sinsimila Soup

Ingredients: Serves 6-8

    3 cups water, hot

    8 oz celery, chopped

    8 oz of broccoli tops or asparagus tips

    2 oz onions, chopped

    ¼ cup bud-butter

    1 tbsp flour

    1/2 cup heavy cream

    1/2 cup bud-milk

Boil water with celery, broccoli or asparagus for five minutes. Sauté the onions in bud-butter until lightly brown. Add flour to onion and butter stir, then add the cream and mix well. Add cream mixture to water with vegetables and simmer for five minutes or until thickens. Do not allow to boil after adding bud-milk.

Fried Wontons

Ingredients: Serves 1-2

    10-12 wontons

    1/8-1/4 cup bud-oil

    2 tbsp water

ADD ENOUGH BUD-OIL TO COVER THE BOTTOM of a small non-stick frying pan and heat on medium high heat. Add wontons and cook until golden brown. Add water, cover, and steam for 30 seconds and serve with sprinkle of soy sauce.

Garlic Salmon Over Spinach

Ingredients: Serves 4

    4 - 4-oz salmon filets

    4 tbsp bud-butter

    6 garlic cloves, minced

    2 tbsp lemon pepper seasoning

    6 oz fresh spinach

MELT BUD-BUTTER IN A LARGE SKILLET over medium-high heat. Stir in 4 cloves of minced garlic. Sprinkle salmon filets on both sides with lemon pepper seasoning. Place the salmon in the pan with the bud-butter sauted garlic and cook on both sides, approximately 3 minutes per side, until fish flakes when tested with a fork.

Steam fresh spinach for approximately 4 minutes or until tender. Toss spinach with remaining 2 cloves of minced garlic. Serve the salmon filets over the spinach.

Marijuana Pesto

Ingredients:

    1/2 cup basil, chopped

    1/4 cup bud-canola oil

    1/3 cup olive oil

    1/2 cup parmesan, grated

    1/2 cup romano cheese, grated

    3 garlic heads, chopped

Mix ALL INGRE-DIENTS IN A FOOD PROCESSOR and refrigerate for at least 24 hours. Serve over lightly cooked pasta or spaghetti. Serve with baked or sautéd salmon.

Sardine, Chickpea & Celery Salad

Ingredients: Serves 4

8 sardines, water or oil packed

4 celery stalks

16 oz can chickpeas, drained and rinsed

¼ cup parsley, chopped

2 tbsp lemon juice

1 tbsp bud-oil

½ tsp ground cumin

¼ tsp salt

Pinch of freshly ground pepper

WASH THE CELERY and trim the tops and bottoms. Cut celery stalks into very thin slices, diagonally. Combine the celery slices with the chickpeas and parsley in a serving bowl. In a small bowl whisk together the lemon juice, bud-oil, cumin, salt and pepper to taste. Toss the salad with the dressing and allow to sit at room temperature for 10-15 minutes to allow the flavors to meld. Remove the sardines from the tin, and break each one into two pieces. Top each individual serving of salad with four sardine pieces. Serve at room temperature.

Hemp Seeds

SHELLED HEMP SEEDS ARE EASY TO DIGEST, packed with proteins, high in omega-3 and GLA. You can use them much the way you would use sesame seeds—sprinkle on salads, cereals, soups, and even on ice cream Sundays.

Marijuana Spaghetti Sauce

Ingredients:

    1 can tomato paste

    ¼ cup bud-canola oil or bud-olive oil or bud-butter

    1/2 cup chopped onions

    6 oz water

    1/2 tsp salt

    1/2 garlic clove, minced

    1 bay leaf

    1 pinch thyme

    1 pinch pepper

MIX INGREDIENTS in a large cooking pot. Cover and simmer for two hours, stirring frequently. Serve over lightly cooked spaghetti.

Spicy Almond Sauce

Ingredients:

   ½ cup raw almond butter

   ¼ cup rice vinegar

   2 tsp agave nectar

   1 tsp ginger, peeled and chopped

   2-3 tbsp crushed red chili flakes to taste

   Sea salt to taste

BLEND the almond butter, rice vinegar, agave, ginger, and crushed red pepper flakes to taste in a food processor or high-speed blender until completely smooth. Add hot water

as needed to reach the desired consistency (about 3 teaspoons). Add salt to taste and adjust seasoning. This sauce can be made in advance and kept in the refrigerator for up to a week.

Spicy Almond Soba Noodles

Ingredients: Serves 2

4 oz buckwheat soba noodles

1 garlic clove, minced

2 tsp fresh ginger, minced

2 scallions, cut into thin slices

½ red bell pepper, seeded, thinly sliced, then chopped

½ cup cabbage, shredded

½ cup broccoli florets, blanched & cut to bite-size pieces

¼ cup almond slivers, toasted

Bud-oil

Spicy almond sauce.

BRING a large pot of water to a boil and add a pinch of salt and a splash of bud-oil. Add the soba noodles and cook until just tender, about 10 minutes. Drain and set aside. In a large sauté pan or wok, heat a splash of bud-oil over high heat. Add the garlic, ginger, cabbage, and broccoli and sauté for 5-10 minutes until desired crispness is reached. Remove vegetables from heat, add the noodles, and toss with the spicy almond sauce, scallions, and red bell pepper. Top with toasted almond slivers and additional sauce.

Desserts & Snacks

Wowie Marijuana Brownies

Ingredients: Makes 36 Brownies

1 cup bud-butter

4 squares of unsweetened baking chocolate

2 cups sugar

4 eggs

1 cup flour

Vanilla extract

Nuts, chopped (optional)

PRE-HEAT OVEN to 350° F and grease 13 x 9 x 2 inch baking pan. Heat bud-butter and chocolate in sauce pan and stir with wooden spoon until smooth. Stir in sugar. Stir in eggs one at a time. Add vanilla extract, nuts, and stir in flour mixture. Spread mixture in pan and bake for 40 minutes. Allow to cool before cutting.

Marshmallow Pecan Brownies

Ingredients: Makes 12 Brownies

 1 package Duncan Hines Snack Size Brownie Mix

 2 tbsp water

 1/4 cup bud-canola oil

 1 large egg

 1 cup mini marshmallows

 1/4 cup pecans, chopped

 Toothpick

PREHEAT OVEN TO 350° F. Grease bottom of 8-inch square pan with bud-butter. In large bowl mix brownie mix, water, oil, and egg and stir until well-blended. Stir in marshmallows and pecans. Pour batter into greased pan and bake for 25-30 minutes. Brownies are done when toothpick inserted 1 inch from edge comes out clean. Cool completely before cutting.

Pot Fudge Pops

Ingredients   Makes 6-8 pops

½ cup bud-milk

3 ½ oz dark chocolate, finely chopped

11 oz açaí juice

1/3 cup agave nectar

Pinch of salt

PLACE the dark chocolate in a bowl and set aside. Heat the bud-milk in a small saucepan for 1-2 minutes, until near boiling. Pour the heated bud-milk over the chocolate. Let sit for a few minutes to allow the chocolate to melt, then stir well, until completely smooth. Pour in the açaí juice, agave nectar, and salt, and mix thoroughly to combine. Cool to room temperature, and pour into pop molds. Place in the freezer and allow at least 4 hours before serving, or until the pops are completely solid.

Soma Cookies

Ingredients

    2 cups flour

    1 1/2 cups oats

    1 1/2 cups light brown sugar

    1 cup granulated sugar

    1 cup bud-butter

    2 eggs

    2 cups pecans, chopped

    1 cup raisons

    1 cup cranberries, dried

    1 tsp salt

    1 tsp baking soda

    2-3 tbsp vanilla

    1 tsp nutmeg, ground

    1 tbsp cinnamon, ground

SIFT DRY INGREDIENTS TOGETHER, except for the oats, and set aside. Cream the bud-butter and sugars, add vanilla and mix in the eggs. Mix dry ingredients into wet ingredients. Mix in oats and blend. Fold in the currants, cranberries, and pecans. Chill the batter. Using small ice cream scooper, drop dough onto greased cookie sheet and bake at 350° F for 15-17 minutes.

Tokers Cookies

Ingredients   Makes 5 dozen cookies

   2 1/4 cups flour

   1 tsp baking soda

   1 tsp salt

   1 cup bud-butter

   3/4 cup sugar

   3/4 cup brown sugar, packed

   1 tsp vanilla

   2 large eggs

   1 3/4 cups chocolate chips

   1 cup nuts, chopped

PREHEAT OVEN TO
375° F. Melt the bud-
butter in a saucepan over
low heat. In a small bowl,
combine the flour, baking
soda, and salt. In a larger
bowl, blend the bud-butter,
sugar, brown sugar, and vanilla until creamy. Blend in

eggs, one at a time, beat. Slowly blend in the flour mixture. Stir
in the chocolate chips and chopped nuts. Drop balls of dough
on to an ungreased baking sheet, about 2 inches apart. Bake for
9-11 minutes, or until golden brown. Cool before removing
cookies.

Quick And Easy Chocolate Chip Cookies

Ingredients: Makes 3 dozen

   1 package chocolate chip cookie mix

   ¼ cup bud-butter

   1/2 cup water

   1 egg

   1 cup mini marshmallows (optional)

   1/2 cup nuts, chopped (optional)

PREHEAT OVEN to 375° F. Grease large cookie sheet. Pour mix into medium bowl, Add egg, bud-butter, and water and mix until smooth. Mix in marshmallows and nuts. Using ice cream scoop, place dough scoops 2 inches apart and bake for 8 to 10 minutes. Cool before removing cookies from sheet.

Cannabis Crisps

Ingredients: Makes 20 Crisps

¼ cup bud-butter

1 - 10 oz bag regular marshmallows

6 cups rice crispy cereal

1 - 12 oz package butterscotch pieces

MELT THE BUD-BUTTER IN A LARGE SAUCEPAN over low heat. Add marshmallows and mix until completely melted and then remove from heat. Quickly add the cereal and mix until coated. Fold in the butterscotch pieces. Press the mixture into a greased 13 x 9 x 2-inch baking pan. Set aside to cool. Cut into 2-inch squares.

Stoney Fudge

Ingredients: Makes 50 squares

  4 cups sugar

  2 - 5 oz cans evaporated milk

  1 cup bud-butter

  1 - 12 oz. package semisweet chocolate chips

  1 - 7 oz. jar marshmallow creme

  1 tsp vanilla

  Candy thermometer

  13 x 9 x 2-inch pan

COMBINE THE SUG-AR, milk, and bud-butter in a large pot. Stirring frequently, cook on medium high until it begins to boil, then reduce to medium heat. Continue to cook and stir for 10-15 minutes, until the temp reaches 236° F. Be careful to not burn mixture. Turn off heat and stir in the chocolate chips, vanilla, and marshmallow creme. Mix until well-blended and smooth. Pour into the pre-buttered dish. Cut into 1 ½ squares.

Leary Biscuit

Ingredients:

    1 Ritz Cracker

    1 tsp butter

    1/2 slice cheese

    1 marijuana bud

Take a Ritz cracker, smear it with butter, add some cheese, and put the marijuana bud on top. Microwave on high for 35-40 seconds, or until the cheese is melted. Allow to cool for 1-2 minutes.

Quick Stoner Biscuit

Ingredients:

> 1-2 cookies or biscuits
>
> 1-2 tbsp bud-butter, heaping

PLACE 1 TO 2 COOKIES or biscuits on plate. Put heaping tablespoon bud-butter on top of each biscuit and heat in microwave for 35 seconds. Cool for 1 minute before eating.

Pop Corn

Ingredients:

>   3 tbsp bud-oil
>
>   1/2 cup popping corn
>
>   2 tbsp bud-butter

PUT the bud-oil in a tall pot and heat over medium-low heat. Put 1-2 kernels in the oil and when they begin to pop, add the rest of the corn. Cover the pot, and shake during popping until the popping noise dies down. Remove the pot from heat. The corn will finish popping. Remove lid and add bud-butter and salt to taste.

Roasted Squash Dip

Ingredients: Serves 8-10

- ½ small pumpkin
- 1 butternut squash
- 2 acorn squashes
- ¼ cup bud-oil
- 1 cup pine nuts
- 1 cup dried cranberries
- 3 tbsp vinegar
- Pinch salt and pepper

PREHEAT OVEN to 450° F. Peel, de-seed, and finely dice pumpkin and squash, and place in a large bowl. Add bud-oil, season to taste with salt and pepper and toss. Spread mixture evenly in a single layer on baking sheets and place in oven and roast about 20-25 minutes until soft, Turn occasionally. Put pine nuts and bud-butter into frying pan. Toast until light brown, turning often. Put roasted squash in a mixing bowl and add toasted pine nuts, cranberries, and vinegar and toss. Refrigerate until chilled. Service with tortilla chips. Makes 3-4 cups.

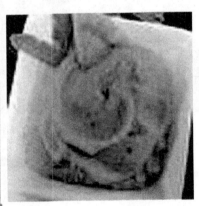

Quick Chocolate Marijuana Icing

Ingredients:

    1-16 oz Betty Crocker Chocolate frosting

    4 tbsp bud-butter, soft

POUR FROSTING INTO MEDIUM BOWL, add bud-butter, and mix until smooth. Ice cake or cookies.

Drinks

Bhang Marijuana Milk

Ingredients:

    2 cups water

    1 oz marijuana

    4 cups milk

    2 tbsp almonds, blanched and chopped

    1/8 tsp cloves, cinnamon, cardamom, mixed

    1/4 tsp ginger, powdered

    3/4 cup sugar

REMOVE SEEDS and twigs from mj and to boiling water in a teapot, cover and simmer for about 7 minutes. Strain through a coffee filter and save the water. Add the chopped almonds and small amount of milk to small bowl and grind with mortar until a fine paste is formed. Squeeze paste through filter and collect the extract. Repeat a few more times until all that is left are some fibers and nut meal. Discard the residue. Combine all the liquids that have been collected, including the water the marijuana was brewed in. Add to this the cloves, cinnamon, cardamom, ginger, sugar and remaining milk and mix well. Chill and serve.

Marijuana Tea

Ingredients:

Your favorite tea bags

1 tsp of bud-butter

1 cup marijuana

Alcohol, spices, honey, milk, mint

BOIL THE WATER, then add the marijuana and let it simmer for about 15 minutes. Add tea bags, bud-butter, milk, honey, and alcohol to taste. The alcohol will greatly enhance the effects of the tea. When adding milk pour it very slowly so it doesn't curdle or you can microwave the milk first so its warm when it hits the boiling tea. Boil for another 5 to 10 minutes. Pour it in a cup and serve.

Marijuana Twig Tea

Ingredients:

    1-2 cups marijuana stems

    2 cups water

GRIND MARIJUANA STEMS INTO A POWDER with a coffee grinder or mortar and pestle. In a saucepan, bring water to a rolling boil. Add the ground up stems, cover, and reduce heat to low. Let steep for 5-10 minutes, and then toss in a tea bag or two of your favorite tea. Let steep another 5 minutes. Strain tea using a tea strainer or coffee filter. Add some or sugar to taste and serve.

Hot Chocolate

Ingredients:

    1 cup bud-milk

    1 cup cream

    4 g marijuana, finely chopped

    5 oz chocolate, unsweetened

    1/2 tsp vanilla

    5 tbsp sugar

    Pinch of salt

    Pinch of cinnamon

COMBINE the bud-milk, sugar, and salt in a saucepan on medium heat. When salt and sugar dissolves, mix in the cream, cinnamon, vanilla, and cannabis. Turn the heat off and add chocolate and stir until melted. Serve in mug with whipped cream or miniature marshmallows.

Soy Smoothie

Ingredients:

    1 1/2 cup ice

    1 cup bud-milk

    1/2 cup strawberries, chopped

    1/3 cup tofu, firm

    2 bananas, ripe, sliced

    1/8 tsp cardamom

BLEND ingredients in blender until smooth. Serve with glob of whipped cream.

Ginger Coffee

Ingredients:

    1/2 cup coffee, ground

    2 tsp cardamom, ground

    3 tsp ginger, fresh, ground

    4 cups water, cold

    1 cup bud-milk

    2 tsp sugar

    Whipped cream

    Chocolate, dark, grated

COMBINE COFFEE, CARDAMOM, GINGER AND BREW with cold water. Combine milk and sugar in small saucepan over low heat, stirring constantly until hot. Whip cream to soft peaks with remaining cardamom. Serve with hot milk, top with dollop of whipped cream and sprinkle with grated chocolate.

Chai-Indian Tea

Ingredients:

4 cup water

4 black tea bags

3 cup bud-milk

1/3 cup honey

4 cinnamon sticks

1/4 tsp cardamom, ground

1 bay leaf

5 cloves, whole

COMBINE ALL INGREDIENTS in medium saucepan and bring to boil. Reduce heat and simmer, uncovered, for 30 minutes. Serve chilled or hot. For more spicy flavor, increase cinnamon, cloves and cardamom proportionally.

Aliments

Anxiety

GENERALIZED ANXIETY DISORDER (GAD) is characterized by excessive, exaggerated anxiety and worry about everyday life events with no obvious reasons for the worry. People with GAD symptoms tend to expect disaster and can't stop worrying about health, money, family, work, or school. In *Worrywart's Companion: Twenty-One Ways to Soothe Yourself and Worry Smart* Docpotter explains how such unrealistic and out of proportion worry gets a hold. Daily life becomes a constant state of worry, fear, and dread. Eventually, anxiety so dominates thinking that it interferes with daily functioning, including work, school, social activities, and relationships. Life becomes a big drag, especially for those around the worrywart.

Worrywart Symptoms

Not only does worrywarting affects the way you think, but the anxiety can lead to physical symptoms, as well. People with run-away anxiety often have other anxiety disorders, like panic attacks, obsessive-compulsive disorder, and phobias, often suffer from depression and abuse drugs or alcohol.

Symptoms of Worrywarting
Excessive, ongoing worry and tension
Unrealistic view of problems
Feeling of being "edgy"
Irritability

Muscle tension
Headaches
Sweating
Difficulty concentrating
Nausea
Frequent visits to bathroom
Feeling tired often
Sleeping problems
Trembling
Easily Startled

How to Soothe Anxiety

Sunshine is a natural anxiety soother. Marijuana is a palliative and is soothing. The two work wonders together. Eat a marijuana edible and sit out in the sun for 15 minutes daily. Watch the birds in your yard. Listen to the grass grow. Don't use sunscreen to naturally increase Vitamin D levels, which can decrease depression and anxiety.

Chamomile

Chamomile is a natural nervous system tonic. It can ease away the overwhelming feelings associated with anxiety and promotes a good nights sleep. Try a cup of Chamomile Tea before bed. Chamomile contains *apigenin* and *luteolin*, both of which promote relaxation. For calming action use two chamomile tea bags to 1 cup of water and steep, covered for 10 minutes. Drink three cups a day.

Kava Kava

Kava Kava is well known for providing an over all sense of calm. It's affects are compared to those of Valium. Kava is a strong herb, and caution needs to be used when drinking Kava tea, but it does ease the symptoms of anxiety and provides for a good nights sleep.

Valerian

Valerian has historically been used to treat insomnia and anxiety. It has a sedative like effect and can greatly ease the symptoms of anxiety and anxiety disorders. Valerian tea is also good for soothing anxiety. Valium is derived from the herb valerian.

Avoid caffeine, which is a psycho-stimulant that stimulates central nervous system and stays in the bloodstream and tissues for up to six hours. Colas, teas, and chocolate are loaded with caffeine. Instead drink chamomile tea, which is the classic remedy for soothing frazzled nerves.

Deep Breathing

Diaphragmatic breathing or deep breathing from the diaphragm rather than the chest automatically relaxes the body and reduces anxiety. Emotions and breathing have a reciprocal relationship, meaning that when you are anxious, nervous or upset your breathing quickens and may even become erratic. When you are relaxed and composed your breathing is slow, calm and rhythmical. By controlling your breath, through regular practice of specific exercises, your mind and your emotions can be calmed.

Find a quiet place free of distractions. Lie on the floor or recline in a chair, loosen tight clothing and remove glasses or contacts. Rest your hands in your lap or on the arms of the chair.

Place one hand on your upper chest and the other hand on your stomach. Inhale, taking a deep breath from your abdomen as you count to three. As you inhale you should feel your stomach rise up. The hand on your chest should not move. After a short pause, slowly exhale while counting to three. Your stomach should fall back down as you exhale. Continue this pattern of rhythmic breathing for five to ten minutes.

To increase the power of your deep breathing, listening to a voice recording, which includes directions on practicing diaphragmatic breathing. Use of an audio recording allows you to fully relax and concentrate on the technique. You can usually find a free download by searching google.

Additionally, you might eat a marijuana edible or drink about an hour before doing the exercise. Try burning a mixture of lavender and hemp oils, which gives off a soothing aroma that will relax you and your brain.

Arthritis

ARTHRITIS IS A DISORDER CHARACTERIZED BY joint inflammation and is usually accompanied by considerable stiffness and pain, called *arthralgia*. Arthritis is a rheumatic disease. There are many forms of arthritis, ranging from wear and tear of cartilage, such as osteoarthritis, to those associated with inflammation as a result of an overactive immune system, such as rheumatoid arthritis.

The causes of arthritis depend on the form, including injury, abnormal metabolism like gout, genetics, infections like Lyme disease, or an overactive immune system like rheumatoid arthritis and systemic lupus erythematosus.

Arthritis Symptoms

Symptoms of arthritis include pain and limited function of joints and surrounding tendons. Inflammation of the joints from arthritis is characterized by joint stiffness, swelling, redness, and warmth. Tenderness of the inflamed joint can be present. Loss of range of motion and deformity can result.

Because they are rheumatic diseases, arthritis, can cause symptoms affecting various organs of the body that do not directly involve the joints. Therefore, symptoms in some patients with certain forms of arthritis can also include fever, gland swelling, weight loss, fatigue, and feeling generally unwell.

Arthritis Treatment

Treatment programs must be customized for the individual patient. Treatment programs can incorporate home remedies, nonprescription and prescription medications, joint injections, and surgical operations. Some treatment programs involve weight reduction and avoiding activities that exert excessive stress on the joint. The goal of treatment of arthritis is to reduce joint pain and inflammation while preventing damage and improving and maintaining joint function.

Because inflammation is usually involved, you would probably benefit from avoiding common fats, including butter. The problem is that many medical marijuana recipes call for bud-butter, which probably increases inflammation. You can avoid this problem by substituting one of oils with ALA or GLA, such an canola oil in preparing bud-oil you use in cooking.

Inflammatory Foods

You can dramatically reduce inflammatory pain by avoiding pro-inflammatory foods, like sodas and sugary juice drinks. Processed sugars and other high-glycemic starches increase inflammation, just as they raise blood sugar, Watch for sugar content in salad dressings, and use them sparingly on salads. Unfortunately many marijuana edibles available in the clubs are made from just these ingredients!

In joint pain the key is to find out what food cause your pain and avoiding them, while eating foods that almost never cause symptoms. Foods commonly identified as triggers for arthritis includes dairy products, wheat, citrus. corn, cornstarch, caffeine, beef, pork, nuts, tomatoes, and eggs.

Add Pain-Soothing Foods

Foods that relieve inflammation help your joints to cool down.
Anti-inflammatory foods include brown rice, cooked or died
fruits, cherries, cranberries, pears, prunes, but not citrus fruits or
apples, bananas, peaches or tomatoes. Other anti-inflammatory
foods include cooked green, yellow or orange vegetables, artichokes, asparagus, broccoli, chard, collards, lettuce, spinach, string
beans, summer or winter squash, sweet potatoes, tapioca, and
plain or carbonated water.

Marijuana

Marijuana contains powerful anti-inflammatory compounds as
well as natural analgesics, providing a one-two punch that makes
medicinal marijuana an excellent part of an arthritis treatment
plan. Medical marijuana can relieve joint pain while at the same
time reducing the inflammation that precipitated that pain. Rheumatoid arthritis and osteoarthritis symptoms be treated with the
help of cannabinoids naturally occurring in marijuana.

Topical Treatments

Hot Wax Dip

Some people get significant relief of pain symptoms by dipping
their hands in the morning in hot wax—paraffin—dips available
from local pharmacies or medical supply stores. Melt the wax in a
crock-pot and cover your hands with warm wax. Peel it off when
harden and return to the pot for future use.

Warm water soaks and wearing nighttime cotton gloves to
keep the hands warm during sleep can also help ease hand symptoms. You might experiment with dipping the gloves in a marijuana tincture , then wearing all night, as a kind of compress. While
you sleep the soothing cannabinoids and other chemicals slowly
enter your body through your skin.

Gentle range of motion exercises performed regularly can help to preserve function of the joints. These exercises are easiest to perform after early morning hand-warming. Magnify the soothing effects by eating a marijuana cookie, brownie, or sipping a cup of marijuana-chamomile tea about an hour before treatment.

Rheumatoid Arthritis Poultice

This recipe is from a patient who suffers debilitating rheumatoid arthritis. She reports complete and rapid pain relief, lasting for about one hour.

Place accumulated stems and scraps of leaves into a five-gallon glass jar. Fill to the top with rubbing alcohol, cover and store in a dark corner for a month or more. It will be much more powerful if left to sit for many months. Pour the dark green solution through a filter screen, then back into the original rubbing alcohol containers. Moisten a washcloth and apply directly to painful joints as a compress or use a spray bottle.

As a quick alternative, mix bud-oil or marijuana tincture with shea butter, cocoa butter or beeswax, instead of rubbing alcohol. Then use as a soothing ointment.

Epsom Salt Bath

Epsom Salt is high in magnesium, which is important for bone growth and regulates the body's pH level. A deficiency of magnesium lowers the ability of the body to absorb and use calcium and phosphorus, which are the two primary bone-building minerals.

An Epsom Salt Bath can be used to reduce the symptoms associated with arthritis. Add three cups of Epsom Salt in hot bath water and soak in it. The magnesium in the salt is absorbed by the body and it soothes and relaxes the stiff joints and muscles. Eat a marijuana edible about an hour before your medicinal bath and/or enjoy a joint while you soak. NOTE: Excessive magnesium can cause diarrhea, nausea, cramps, muscle weakness, and heart abnormalities.

Use Flax Seed Oil

Flax seed oil's primary ingredient is Omega-3 fat, which helps the body produce prostaglandins—anti-inflammatory hormone-like molecules. These molecules help reduce the inflammation associated with rheumatoid arthritis and osteoarthritis. Flax seed is believed by many to be a natural cure for arthritis. Instead of butter or olive oil, try using flax seed oil as the basis for cannabinoid extraction. Then simply take one tablespoon of infused flax seed oil three times daily. Continue this remedy for at least one month to improve primary forms of arthritis.

For breakfast, add flax seeds to your cereal, muffin, or bread, or mix ground flax seeds plus hemp seeds into chocolate/strawberry milk or orange juice. For lunch and dinner, flax and hemp seeds can be ground and sprinkled directly onto almost any meal.

Alfalfa Seeds

A tea made from alfalfa, especially from its seeds, has shown beneficial results in the treatment of arthritis. Simply add one teaspoon of alfalfa seeds to one cup of boiling water. Take three to four cups of this tea daily for approximately two weeks to reduce inflammation. Another option is to regularly take alfalfa capsules or add a small amount of alfalfa to your diet.

Cinnamon

Recent studies have shown that cinnamon is a remarkable natural treatment for arthritis pain. Simply add half a teaspoon of cinnamon powder to one tablespoon of honey and stir into a cup of bud-milk every morning before breakfast. Repeat this daily for one month. Results should be noticeable within the first week.

Marijuana Pain-Relief Cocktail

Ingredients:

    1 cup carrot

    1 cup celery

    3/4 cup beets

    3/4 cup cucumbers

    1 tsp parsley

    4 drops marijuana tincture

BLEND VEGETABLES WELL IN JUICER and add marijuana tincture and mix well. Drink 8 to 16 ounces daily when arthritis flares up.

Canna-Cod Liver Oil

Research has shown that consuming a small amount of cod liver oil each day can potentially slow down cartilage degeneration, which is one of the main symptoms of osteoarthritis. Additionally, the omega-3 acids contained in the oil can help reduce the pain and inflammation associated with arthritis. Therefore, simply consuming 1 to 2 teaspoons of cod liver oil daily could be very beneficial.

You can create your own cod liver concoction by adding 1/4 cup of finely ground marijuana bud to bottle of cod liver oil and leaving in a dark place for several weeks.

Studies have shown that if you suffer from repetitive strain injuries, a cod oil pack can help. Dose cloth into the cod oil that has been infused with marijuana, place the pack on strained area, wrap in plastic wrap, then wrap in a dry cloth, and heat with a heating pad for 45 minutes. Canna-castor oil is absorbed right into the skin and into the area of inflammation and reduces inflammation tremendously.

Turmeric

Trumeric is a common spice in Indian cuisine that has been used to reduce inflammation for hundreds of years in Ayurvedic medicine. By taking 500 mg. to 1000 mg. Turmeric capsules three times per day, many individuals have reported significant relief from osteoarthritis pain. The spice can be added to many recipes and infused into bud-oils.

Ginger

Similar to Turmeric, the common kitchen spice. Ginger has been found to be an effective natural anti-inflammatory. Therefore, a great remedy for arthritis is to peel and slice 1/2 inch of fresh ginger and take it with each meal. Alternatively the ginger can be boiled in a small amount of water to make tea. Then sweetened with tablespoon of honey and bud-milk.

Headaches

A MIGRAINE HEADACHE is a form of vascular headache. It is caused by vasodilatation or enlargement of blood vessels. Enlargement of these blood vessels stretch the nerves that coil around them and causes the nerves to release chemicals. The chemicals cause inflammation, pain, and further enlargement of the artery. The increasing enlargement of the arteries magnifies the pain.

Migraines are often triggered by eating certain foods. Common offenders include alcohol, especially beer and red wine; aged cheeses; chocolate; aspartame; overuse of caffeine; monosodium glutamate; salty foods; and processed foods. Skipping meals or fasting also can trigger migraine attacks. Milk products are high on the list of offenders, including milk chocolate so medical marijuana patients need to pay attention to the edibles because so often they are made of sugar and chocolate, both of which are among the food offenders in many cases causing pain.

Stress can instigate migraines. Bright lights and sun glare can induce migraines, as can loud sounds. Unusual smells—including pleasant scents, such as perfume, and unpleasant odors, such as paint thinner and secondhand smoke—can also trigger migraines. Changes in wake-sleep pattern. Missing sleep or getting too much sleep may serve as a trigger for migraines in some individuals, as can jet lag. Certain medications can aggravate migraines, especially oral contraceptives and vasodilators, such as nitroglycerin.

Triptans are the primary medical treatment for migraines. They work by narrowing arteries in the head. The problem is that they also narrow arteries in the heart, which makes them potentially dangerous in some people because of the risk of heart attack or stroke. This poses a risk for seemingly healthy adults whose atherosclerosis and narrowing of the coronary arteries is "silent", that is, without past strokes, transient ischemic attacks, heart attacks, or angina.

Identify the Cause

Many tension headaches are brought about by some trigger. Common triggers include stress, depression, hunger, dehydration, menstruation, eye strain staring at your computer, tobacco smoke, alcohol, A/C being on heat for a long time, and certain foods. If you get frequent headaches, consider keeping a headache diary to help you to identify potential triggers so that you can avoid them.

Avoid the Trigger

If you think you know what triggered your headache, avoid that thing. If it's stress, for example, remove yourself from the stressful situation and do a relaxation exercise, like breathing deeply. If the sun's bright light is aggravating your headache, go inside or put on sunglasses. You can't get away from some triggers, such as a food that you already ate, but you can avoid them in the future.

Relax

Relaxing can help speed up your recovery even if your headache isn't caused by tension. Meditate, do some yoga, sit quietly and breath slowly and deeply, listen to soothing music, take a warm bath.

Take a Nap

Sleeping is one of the best treatments for headaches. Just lying down and resting your eyes speeds relief.

Drink Water

Dehydration is a common cause of headaches, and even if you don't feel thirsty, you may benefit from a glass or two of water.

Drink Coffee

Caffeine is a vasoconstrictor so it constricts the blood vessels, which can lessen head pain. Drink a Cup O' Joe. Sip a can of cola.

Massage Your Temples

Simply applying a little pressure to the most painful area or rubbing your head in that vicinity will sometimes provide temporary relief. Using bud-oil to massage your jaw, neck, and shoulders is soothing and relieves tension. The cannabinoids in the oil are absorbed through the skin into the bloodstream.

Cayenne pepper balms, oils, and creams are *rubefacients*, which are herbs that warm the body by quickly dilating small capillaries, increasing circulation, which reddens the skin. Indeed, cayenne's most prominent attribute is increased circulation, and stimulation to the heart and lungs. Cayenne s often added to herbal formulas activate and complement other herbs, including marijuana.

For a quickie pain-reducing poultice, add just enough bud-oil to 2-3 tablespoons cayenne pepper powder to create a paste. Put the pepper-bud paste on the aching area. Lay back, breathe deeply, imagine the pain receding—floating away.

Smile

Smiling can work wonders if it's just a minor headache. Smiling releases endorphins within the brain as it works on a positive feedback loop—the more you smile, the more "feel-good" chemicals the brain releases, and the more of these chemicals it releases, the more you smile! Endorphins help to relieve the pain. Toke up and giggle!

Eat a Sweet

For some people, eating something sweet, like a marijuana cookie or cupcake, decreases their painful headaches when they then lie down and sleep. This only works if you normally don't eat many sweet things during the day.

Marijuana Headache Relief Tonic

Ingredients:

    1 tsp yarrow, finely chopped

    1 tsp peppermint, finely chopped

    1 tsp honey

    5 drops marijuana tincture

POUR BOILING WATER OVER YARROW and peppermint. Cover and allow to steep for 3 to 5 minutes. Stir in honey and drink.

Multiple Sclerosis

MULTIPLE SCLEROSIS (MS) PATIENTS get burning pain in the legs and muscle stiffness and spasms that keep them awake at night. MS is a disease in which the nerves of the central nervous system—brain and spinal cord—degenerate. Myelin, which covers and insulates nerves, aiding in the conduction of impulses along the nerves is important for maintaining the health of the nerves. In MS, inflammation causes the myelin to degenerate. Consequently, the electrical impulses that travel along the nerves decelerate and slow. In addition, the nerves themselves are damaged. As more and more nerves are affected, you experience a progressive interference with functions controlled by the nervous system like vision, speech, walking, writing, and memory.

The cause of multiple sclerosis is unknown. In recent years, researchers have focused on the immune system and genetics. Researchers suspect that a foreign agent such as a virus alters the immune system so that it perceives myelin as an intruder and attacks it. The attack by the immune system on the tissues that it is supposed to protect is called *autoimmunity*, and multiple sclerosis is believed to be a disease of autoimmunity. While some of the myelin may be repaired after the assault, some of the nerves are stripped of their myelin covering and become demyelinated.

Tests on cell cultures and lab animals have revealed that CBD fights inflammation. It is thought that CBD's anti-inflammatory effect works, at least in some cases, through its antioxidant properties, which is the ability to soak up highly reactive molecules called *free radicals*, which cause cell damage.

The pain, stiffness and some balance problems are usually reduced when inflammation is controlled. The easiest way to control inflammation is by altering diet. Eliminate inflammatory causing foods, like sugar and processed foods, and adding pain-soothing foods, like brown rice, cooked or died fruits, cherries, cranberries, pears, prunes, but not citrus fruits or apples, bananas, peaches or tomatoes. Other anti-inflammatory foods include cooked green, yellow or orange vegetables, artichokes, asparagus, broccoli, chard, collards, lettuce, spinach, string beans, summer or winter squash, sweet potatoes, tapioca, and plain or carbonated water. Eat deep sea fish, which are rich in Omega 3 oils, three to five times a week.

Use cayenne pepper liberally because the capsaicin in it reduces the transmission of pain. You can mix it into stews and sprinkle on salads and meals. Alternatively you can take cayenne pepper caps with each meal. Cayenne pepper extracts are an effective herbal treatment for muscle and joint pain as well as nerve pain caused by shingles, diabetic neuropathy, and MS. It acts by decreasing the chemical used by nerve cells to transmit pain signals. It takes repeated use over a period of at least a few weeks to feel this benefit. Cayenne is also rich in salicylates, which is a natural aspirin-like compound.

Apply cayenne hemp oil to an injury to quickly stimulate circulation and reduce pain. Dip a cloth into cayenne hemp oil and use as a compress. Wrap the cloth around the painful area for 20 to 30 minutes. You can increase the power of the compress by heating the cayenne hemp oil-infused cloth in a microwave. Be careful when it is hot. Alternatively, cover the compress with a cloth and heat with a heating pad.

Cayenne Pain-Relieving Hemp Oil

Ingredients:

    5 tbsp cayenne pepper powder

    ¼ cup powdered marijuana

    2 cups hemp oil

    Glass jar with tightly fitting lid

MIX CAYENNE PEPPER AND MARIJUANA into hemp oil in glass jar. Seal with lid and shake. Place in a warm sunny window for 30 days, shaking daily. Alternatively use a steady source of low heat, like a crock pot, for two weeks, stirring frequently. Strain mixture through muslin, or coffee filter, and rebottle for use. Cayenne hemp oil makes a great base for balms. To make a "icy/hot" oil add menthol crystals to oil while still warm enough to melt the crystals. Watch out for the fumes!

Bladder Control

Bladder hyper-reflexia is a common problem in neurological disorders such as MS. This symptom can be inhibited by cannabinoids. IP 751, a potent synthetic analog of a metabolite of THC effectively suppresses pain and bladder over-activity in hypersensitive bladder disorders such as interstitial cystitis (IC), according to animal model study results presented at the International Continence Society.

IP 751 is a potent anti-inflammatory and a powerful analgesic, although the mechanisms by which it works are unknown. Researchers at the University of Pittsburgh School of Medicine showed that IP 751 significantly suppressed bladder over-activity in animals without affecting bladder contractility. By stopping the underlying cause of irritation, over-activity of the bladder, IP 751 is able to eliminate the associated pain.

Neuroprotection

Cannabinoidal treatment can benefit those suffering neurological disease by slowing the progression in neurodegenerative disorders. Neurodegeneration is central in diseases like Huntington's, Parkinson's, Alzheimer's, MS, and stroke. Although the pathways leading to neuron death will be different in these disorders, there are similarities, such as glutamate-induced excitotoxicity and damage from reactive oxygen and toxic ion imbalances, which may make damaged or demyelinated axons particularly vulnerable. CB1 slows the neurodegenerative effects.

The central nervous system is plastic and can accommodate significant nerve loss before the development of symptoms. Agents that slow this process may have a great effect on the rate of disability in chronic neurodegenerative disease. There is experimental evidence of activity in inflammatory-mediated neurodegeneration, including experimental MS models.

There are indications that cannabinoids can be used in synergistic combination with opioids and benzodiazepines in pain relief. Through combination, opioid doses can be reduced with the advantage of reducing side-effects.

The main function of the endocannabinoid system is to regulate synaptic neurotransmission. The CB1 endocannabinoid system regulates synaptic neurotransmission of excitatory and inhibitory circuits. Endocannabinoids regulate synaptic neurotransmission—neurotransmission, and experimental evidence shows that cannabinoids affect the activity of most neurotransmitters.

Neurotransmitter Functions Under Cannabinoid Control

Neurotransmitter	Associated Disorder
Excitatory Amino Acids	
Glutamate	Epilepsy, nerve-cell death in stroke
Inhibitory Amino Acids	
GABA	Spinal cord motor disorders, epilepsy, anxiety
Glycine	Startle syndromes
Monamines	
Noradrenaline	Automatic homoeostasis, hormones, depression
Serotonin	Depression, anxiety, migraine
Dopamine	Parkinson's disease, schizophrenia, vomiting, Pituitary hormones, drug addiction
Acetylcholine	Neuromuscular disorders, parkinsonism, epilepsy, stay-awake cycle
Neuropeptides	Pain, movement, neural development, anxiety

Table credit: The Therapeutic Potential of Cannabis, David Baker, Gareth Pryce, Gavin Giovannoni, Alan J. Thompson, The Lancet Neurology, Vol. 2, #5, pg 291-298, May 2003.

Use Tinctures

A good way to use marijuana to slow the nerve degeneration associated with MS and other neurological disease is through the use of tinctures. Use an eye dropper or spray to deliver the tincture under the tongue where it is quickly absorbed into the blood stream, by-passing the digestive system.

Alternatively, you might experiment with capsules. You can create several hundred in a batch and with practice determine the best dose for you. Marijuana medicine taken in capsules does go through the digestive system and takes longer to deliver it's effects. Be sure to titrate the best so you don't overdose yourself and experience because once you swal- capsules, you can't get them out of system.

Asthma

ASTHMA IS AN INFLAMMATORY DISORDER of the airways, which causes attacks of wheezing, shortness of breath, chest tightness, and coughing. The exact cause of asthma isn't known. Researchers think certain genetic and environmental factors interact to cause asthma. These factors include: an inherited tendency to develop allergies, called atopy (AT-o-pe), parents who have asthma, contact with airborne allergens or exposure to some viral infections in infancy or in early childhood when the immune system is developing.

The immediate cause of an asthmatic attack is tightening of the muscular bands that regulate the size of the bronchial tubes. These muscles are controlled by nerves, but what triggers the nerves to make airways constrict inappropriately is not clear. The triggers for asthma can be primarily allergic or primarily emotional or induced by exercise or respiratory infection, or it can occur with no obvious causes. It is now being considered an inflammatory disorder.

The airways in people with asthma are always inflamed and very sensitive, so they react to a variety of external factors, or "triggers." Coming into contact with these triggers is what causes an asthma attack—the airways tighten and become inflamed, mucus blocks the airways and results in a worsening of asthma symptoms. A primary way to avoid asthma attacks, which can be life-threatening, is to avoid the triggers.

Avoid Asthma Triggers

Being proactive in taking steps to reduce exposure to things that trigger asthma symptoms is central to controlling asthma attacks.

Clean Your Air. Minimize contact with respiratory irritants, such as smoke, dust, molds, and volatile chemicals. Change the filters in your furnace and air conditioner annually according to the manufacturer's instructions. You might install a small-particle filter in the ventilation system. An air filter your bedroom is helpful so that you breathe filtered air at night. An alternative is to use a negative ion generator, which causes particles to bond with the ions and fall from the air. Medical studies have shown that negative ionic air is beneficial for asthma and other allergies. Use a dehumidifier, which reduces dust mite infestation.

Air conditioning helps to remove airborne pollen from trees, grasses and weeds that gets indoors. Air conditioning lowers indoor humidity and can reduce dust mites in your home. Keep your windows closed during pollen season if you don't have an air conditioner.

Reduce dust. Minimize dust that can worsen nighttime symptoms by encasing pillows, mattresses and box springs in dust-proof covers. Remove carpeting and install hardwood or linoleum flooring. Use washable curtains and blinds. Bath your pets regularly to reduce amount of dander in your surroundings.

Alternative Treatment

Asthma is generally treated with a variety of powerful pharmaceutical drugs, like steroids delivered through an inhaler. There's evidence that certain alternative treatments can help with asthma symptoms. However, keep in mind that these treatments are not a replacement for medical treatment—especially if you have severe asthma. Talk to your doctor before taking any herbs or supplements, as some may interact with medications you take. While some alternative remedies are used for asthma, in most cases more research is needed to see how well they work and to measure the extent of possible side effects.

Breathing and Relaxation Techniques. Yoga classes increase fitness and reduce stress, which may help with asthma as well. Techniques such as meditation, biofeedback, hypnosis and progressive muscle relaxation may help with asthma by reducing tension and stress.

Herbal remedies. A few herbal remedies that have shown some promise in treating asthma symptoms include butterbur, dried ivy and ginkgo extract. Blends of different types of herbs are commonly used in traditional Chinese, Indian and Japanese medicine.

Omega-3 fatty acids found in fish, flaxseed and other foods can reduce the inflammation that leads to asthma symptoms. You might experiment with using flax seed oil instead of olive oil or butter when extracting THC and cannabinoids.

Diet Management

Sugar and fat are major offenders for many asthmatics. Junk foods and sweets certainly are more of a threat than is commonly appreciated. Avoid them like the plague. Dr. Andrew Weil described treating a 12 year old boy for asthma, who was not responding. When he took him off colas, which the boy drank often, the asthma ended. Eat plenty of fruits and vegetables every day.

Medical Marijuana

THC has been shown to cause modest short-term expansion of the air passages in some asthma suffers. However, regular smoking of marijuana joints can lead to chronic cough and airway inflammation. Smokers who smoke both marijuana and tobacco are more than twice as likely than nonsmokers to get respiratory disease and almost three times more likely to contract COPD, according to a Canadian study. However, the same study found that smoking only marijuana was not associated with an increased risk of respiratory symptoms or COPD.

Research shows that the effects of a marijuana cigarette (2 percent THC) or oral delta-9-THC (15 mg), respectively approximately correspond to those obtained with therapeutic does of common bronchodilators drugs (salbutamol, isoprenaline). Following inhalation, the effect lasted about two hours after the joint and about 4 hours after consuming the oral THC. Since inhalation of marijuana products may irritate the mucous membranes, oral administration, such as use of tincture or edibles, is preferable. Very few patients developed brochoconstriction after inhalation of THC.

Native American Method

Lobelia (*Lobelia inflata*), also called Indian tobacco, has a long history of use as an herbal remedy for respiratory conditions such as asthma, bronchitis, pneumonia, and cough. Dr. Andrew Weil suggests using an Indian tobacco or lobelia tincture for acute asthma attacks. Native Americans used lobelia to treat respiratory and muscle disorders, and as a purgative. Today it is used to treat asthma and as an aid in smoking cessation programs. It is a physical relaxant, and can serve as a nerve depressant, easing tension and panic.

Lobelia Pepper Pot Tincture

For acute attacks, try lobelia, or Indian tobacco. Mix three parts tincture of lobelia with one part tincture of capsicum from cayenne pepper and one part tincture of marijuana. Take twenty drops of the mixture in water at the start of an asthmatic attack. Repeat every thirty minutes for a total of three or four doses.

Today, lobelia is often recommended to help clear mucus from the respiratory tract, including the throat, lungs, and bronchial tubes. Although few studies have evaluated the safety and effectiveness of lobelia, some herbalists use lobelia as part of a comprehensive treatment plan for asthma.

Hot Marijuana Linseed Poultice

Many people with asthma get relief from applying a hot marijuana linseed poultice over the front and back of the chest. A poultice can be prepared by mixing one cup or sixteen tablespoons of the linseeds with a quantity of hot water, sufficient to convert them into a moist mealy mass then kneed 3 tbsp bud-oil into the linseed mush.

Get comfortable, lay back, carefully apply the poultice to your chest, and relax, while imagining the beneficial medicines being absorbed through your skin and penetrating and soothing your lungs.

Diet

For long term control and prevention Dr. Andrew Weil recommends decreasing protein intact and replacing animal protein with plant protein whenever possible. Eliminate milk and milk products, substituting other calcium sources. Eat plenty of fruits and vegetables. Eliminate polyunsaturated vegetable oils, margarine, vegetable shortening, all partially hydrogenated oils that might contain trans-fatty acids, all foods that might contain trans-fatty acids (such as deep-fried foods).

Use extra-virgin olive oil as your main fat. Increase intake of omega-3 fatty acids. Make sure to drink plenty of water to keep your respiratory tract secretions more fluid. Slowly, and one at a time, eliminate wheat, corn, soy and sugar for a few weeks each and notice if the condition improves. Eat ginger, turmeric, and marijuana edibles regularly for their anti-inflammatory effects.

Stress

STRESS IS A PHYSICAL RESPONSE to certain encounters with the environment. Your body does many things automatically. You don't have to think to breathe or blink, for example. These automatic responses make up your "basic operating system." When you encounter a stressor, your basic operating system responds with what is called the *general adaptation syndrome*. In the chart you can see that there are three stages: alarm, resistance or adaptation, and exhaustion.

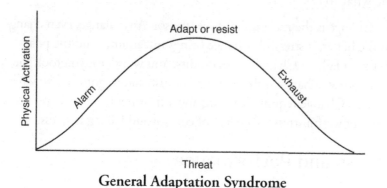

General Adaptation Syndrome

During the alarm stage, the body activates, preparing to fight or flee. Meeting this demand requires physiological changes in the adrenal cortex, hormone secretions, heart rate, breathing, and muscle tension. The energy demand on the body is tremendous and exacts a toll called *stress*.

Out of self-preservation, you move into the second stage: resistance or adaptation where you resist the stressor while seeking a way to nullify it. The level of physical activation drops somewhat from the peak reached during alarm and continues at a moderately high level.

During the resistance phase you search for ways to influence the world in ways you want. When you are successful in dealing with the stressor, functioning becomes easier and activation drops back to its former maintenance level. But when the stressor continues unchanged, activation level remains high.

What Causes Stress?

Things that stress you are called *stressors*. Many stressors are universal. For example, fear and anxiety are stressors. Loud noise, like low-flying airplanes, screaming of sirens, and jack-hammering in the street are stressors. Anything that threatens your safety is a stressor. Some stressors are learned. For example, some people become very agitated when they must give a speech or tell someone what to do.

Change is the most ubiquitous stressor. Any change, even change for the better, is stressful. Change brings uncertainty and the possibility of failure. Change raises doubts. You wonder if you took the right course. Change is threatening because you might not like what happens Change requires learning and adjustment to new conditions. Other powerful stressors are loss of control and feeling helpless.

Stress and Performance

Activation level is the degree of activity in your basic operating system that includes heart and respiratory rates and muscle tension. Understanding the relationship between activation level and performance is central to managing stress. Notice that when activation is low, when you're bored or drowsy, for example, quality of performance suffers. A similar drop in performance occurs when activation is high, when you feel panicky, for example. A moderate level of activation is optimal for peak performance.

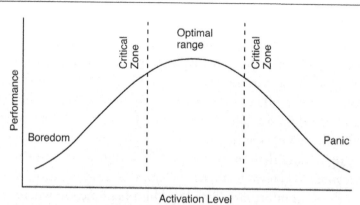

Activation Level and Performance

Sensing Tension

Ability to sense tension from moment to moment is essential to managing stress. "Oh, I know when I'm stressed out." you may say. But this is not always the case. In fact, most people do not accurately read their tension level and are not aware of how inaccurate they can be. To illustrate this, try the following experiment:

Tense-Fist Experiment

Procedure: Make a very tight fist with your left hand and continue holding it tightly for 60 seconds.

Observe: Notice the sensations in your left hand. Notice what you feel, where you feel it, and how intensely you feel it.

Procedure: Continue to hold your left hand in a tight fist for 60 seconds. Then, while still holding your left hand in the tight fist, make another very tight fist with your right combined with the repeated failure to control the situation is experienced first as frustration. If there is no way to turn off the stressor, the frustration turns into futility. Soon comes exhaustion, the third stage of the stress response. Stress wears down your physical hand.

Observe: Notice the sensations in your right hand. Compare the way that your right hand feels with how your left hand feels.

If you're like most people, you probably noticed that the strength of the sensations dropped as you continued applying tension to your left hand. That is, when you first made a fist in your left hand the sensations of tension were very strong but the sensations dropped off considerably in only 60 seconds of holding your hand in a tight fist. The contrast became evident when you made a fist with your right hand: the sensations were much stronger in the right hand than in the left one. This is generally the case for everyone. When we first tense our muscles it feels uncomfortable, but the discomfort rapidly fades. This phenomenon where sensations diminish is called adaptation.

However, because sensations of tension can drop off, it is easy to misread tension levels and miss a vital stress-warning signal. It's much like driving your car with a broken temperature indicator. You know how serious that can be!

Studying Tension and Relaxation

INSTRUCTIONS: Find a place where you can be comfortable and won't be disturbed for about a half hour. Lying on your bed, couch, or a futon on the floor is good. Alternatively, you can sit in an overstuffed chair. Kick off your shoes and loosen your belt and any tight clothing.

Tense and relax each muscle, one at a time, as follows. With eyes closed, tighten the muscle just enough to notice the tension. It is important to learn to detect light tension, so do not tense tightly. While holding the tension for about seven seconds (except for the feet—hold these for three seconds), study the physical sensation of tension in the muscle.

Next, quickly release the tension from the muscle and relax it as much as you can. Study the sensation of relaxation for ten or more seconds. Compare the sensation of relaxation and tension. Then tighten the muscle just enough to notice the tension a second time. Again, study how and where the tension feels for you and compare the feeling of tension to the feeling of relaxation. Then quickly release the tension and relax the muscle as much as you can. Study the way relaxation feels and compare that feeling to the way that the tension felt.

ARMS AND HANDS

Hand and forearm: Make a fist.

Biceps: Bend the arm at the elbow, make a "he-man" muscle.

FACE AND THROAT

Face: Squint eyes, wrinkle nose, and try to pull your whole face into a point at the center.

Forehead: Knit or raise eyebrows.

Cheeks: While clenching the teeth, pull the corners of your mouth to your ears.

Nose and upper lip: With mouth slightly open, slowly bring upper lip down to lower lip.

Mouth: Bring lips together into a tight point, then press mouth into teeth. Blow out gently to relax.

Mouth: Press the right corner of your mouth into your teeth and push the corner slowly toward the center of your mouth. Repeat for the left corner.

Lips and tongue: With teeth slightly apart press lips together and push tongue into top of mouth.

Chin: With arms crossed over chest, stick out your chin and turn it slowly as far as it will go to the left. Repeat for right side.

Neck: Push your chin into your chest at the same time as pushing your head backward into the back of your chair to create a counter-force.

UPPER BODY

Shoulders: Attempt to touch your ears with your shoulders.

Upper back: Push shoulder blades together and stick out chest.

Chest: Take a deep breath.

Stomach: Pull stomach into spine or push it out.

LOWER BODY

Buttocks: Tighten buttocks and push into chair.

Thighs: Straighten leg and tighten thigh muscles.

Calves: Point toes toward your head.

Toes: Curl your toes.

It is important that you tense only the muscles in the area that you are studying while keeping other muscles relaxed. For example, to tense your biceps you bend your arms at the elbow and make a "he-man" muscle. While doing this let your hands hang limp. If you make a fist at the same time that you bend your arm and make the "he-man" muscle, you are tensing two muscle groups rather than one. Doing this makes it harder to study the sensation of tension in the biceps.

Remember, the idea is to discriminate between two feelings—tension and relaxation—so that you can recognize each. It is something like holding a heavy rock in one hand and a lighter rock in the other and "weighing" the two. Discriminating a very heavy rock from a much lighter one is easy. But if you work at it you can eventually learn to identify small differences in weight. The way that you do this is by comparing one against the other. To train yourself to identify small amounts of tension, you study the sensations in a tense muscle, then compare that feeling to how the muscle feels when relaxed.

It takes about twenty-five minutes to go through your entire body slowly and systematically tensing and relaxing your muscles. You must practice to learn to discriminate, so do the exercise or segments of it as often as possible. The more you practice, the better your internal monitor will become.

How to Relax

Relaxation is the opposite of high activation or stress. The biological processes occurring during relaxation allow the body to repair, rest, and prepare for optimal functioning. With practice anyone can learn to relax and use it at specific times to control stress. Personal power increases when you can relax at will. For example, when faced with a crisis situation, if you can keep activation within the optimal range for peak functioning you will remain alert and have all your resources to draw on to deal with the situation. Confidence grows because you know you can remain cool regardless of provocation. You feel in command instead of helpless. In this way ability to manage stress contributes to personal power.

Breathing

Deep breathing is one of the easiest and fastest ways to reduce stress. Slow, steady, smooth, deep breathing will immediately lower activation level. Many people breathe shallowly, which is incorrect because all the air is not forced out of the lungs. During inhalation the diaphragm contracts and descends, increasing lung capacity. During exhalation the diaphragm relaxes and moves upward, forcing the air out. If you are breathing correctly your abdomen should go out when you breathe in. When you breathe out the abdomen should go in. Check to see if you are breathing properly by placing your hand on your abdomen and noticing what happens as you breathe. Does your hand go out when you inhale and in when you exhale?

Anytime you notice yourself getting overly excited or feel tense, you can relax with a few minutes of deep breathing.

Use Your Imagination

Your imagination can be a powerful stress-management tool. Stress can be lowered quite rapidly by taking a few deep breaths and imagining a pleasant fantasy. It is best to have a well- developed fantasy to call on rather than to ad-lib. Waiting until a threatening situation is upon you to select a pleasant fantasy is risky. The situation may overwhelm you before you're able to think up an effective pleasant fantasy.

When a pleasant fantasy has been well-rehearsed, you know exactly what to imagine and can turn to it immediately. A pleasant fantasy can be anything: a real situation, such as hanging in a hammock in your backyard, or an invented one such as riding on a billowy white cloud. There need be no limits. The only requirement is that imagining it relaxes you.

Writing Your Fantasy

Select a situation that you find relaxing for your pleasant fantasy. Review the fantasy in your mind and then write down one or two paragraphs describing the fantasy in detail. Describe the setting. Add as much detail as you can about what it looks like and what is there. Think in terms of the five senses. What do you see? Hear? Feel? Smell? Taste? Add these to the description. For example, if your fantasy is lying on the beach on a warm summer day, you might see the waves, sun, and other sunbathers; hear the waves lapping the shore and seagulls screeching; feel the warmth of the sun and the blanket under you; smell the salty water; and taste a cool soda. The more the fantasy stimulates your senses the more power it will have to relax you.

After imaging your fantasy for two or three minutes stop and add more detail to the written description of the fantasy scenario. What did you find in your fantasy that you did not write on the paper? Add these to the description. This is your pleasant fantasy. You can use it to reduce your tension.

Your pleasant fantasy must be powerful to be effective in quieting tension in difficult situations. You can increase the power of your fantasy by adding details from all the senses and by associating it with deep relaxation. The good time to work on the power of your fantasy is at the end of the deep-muscle-relaxation-training sessions. When you have systematically relaxed all of your muscles and are deeply relaxed, then bring your fantasy to mind. Project yourself into the situation and make it as vivid as you can. Remember to notice what you experience in each sense. Notice how relaxed you feel.

The more often you imagine yourself in the pleasant fantasy, the more relaxing power the fantasy will have. Slowly transfer use to your daily life by following the same gradual procedure used to generalize the relax command.

Music

Most people don't realize that mood can be altered faster with music than with drugs. Try a simple experiment. Look through your collection of cassettes or CDs and select an instrumental with a simple, repetitive melody and a slow, even beat. Then select a second piece that has a fast, changing beat with a strong percussion emphasis, the more chaotic the better. Relax yourself until you feel calm. Play the low-load music and notice your internal reactions. How does it feel? What is your activation level? After a minute stop the music and relax again. Now play the high-load music and notice how you respond. Most likely you noticed a sizable increase in activation in less than a minute when listening to the music with a fast beat.

Music pulls our heart strings. We respond both physically and emotionally. You might feel nostalgia when listening to Pomp and Circumstance, like dancing when listening to a disco tune, or maudlin listening to a love song. Celia might increase her efficiency filling out the report forms if she had a radio in her office and switched it to an upbeat station. The high-load music would bring her activation up to the optimal range and the increased alertness would help her perform at her peak. On the other hand, work requiring intense concentration can raise activation dangerously high. Here Celia would do better to turn the dial to a station that plays calming music because low-load music lowers activation level.

Baths

Baths are another age-old method of modulating body tempo. Stretching out in a tepid bath will relax you every time. Alternatively, when you need to be perked up it is best to take a cold shower. For instance, if you have trouble getting started in the morning you might take a cold shower first thing. Or, if you are tense when you arrive home after work, a warm leisurely bath or dip in a hot tub will probably do the trick.

Food

Food is a powerful regulating tool. Spicy or unusual food are stimulating, whereas bland and familiar foods, like mashed potatoes, have the opposite effect. A quick look through an herb and tea book suggests alternatives to drugs. Cayenne pepper and ginseng, for example, are two natural stimulants; milk and valerian tea are relaxants.

Exercise

Exercise is a popular method of regulating activation level. When you are bored or depressed, vigorous exercise is a very good way of picking yourself up. On the other hand, when you are already highly stressed, a mild light exercise such as a walk around the block will help release tension so you can relax.

Depression

WHEN DEPRESSED, emptiness and despair take hold. Depression makes it tough to do things or to enjoy life. You feel down, low, with no energy. Hobbies and friends don't interest you. You're exhausted and can barely get through the day. Things seem hopeless. Depression is a slippery slope. If you are also suffering pain, such as from MS or arthritis, then it is all that much worse. The pain is worse and the depression is worse.

Causes of depression are not fully understood. For any particular person, the causes may be an inherited propensity, or learned from parents in childhood, or a response to an event like death or job loss to mention a few factors. Usually there are multiple factors in operation, such as a divorce plus having learned to get depressed when disappointed, for example. Sometimes a depressive episode can appear to come out of nowhere at a time when everything seems to be going fine. Other times, depression may be directly related to a significant event, such as losing a loved one, experiencing trauma, or battling an illness. Sometimes depression is a passing sadness, other times it won't let go of you. Chronic depression can actually change your body chemistry to reduce serotonin production, for example, so that your depression becomes self-promoting.

Depression affects both the body and mind. You can't wish it away or snap out of it—although some folks pretend they are happy to hide their depression because they think it is a sign of a weak character.

While each person expresses depression differently, depression has common signs and symptoms. Feelings of helplessness and hopelessness can be overwhelming, along with a loss of interest in daily activities, including hobbies you love and even sex. You seem to have lost your ability to feel joy and pleasure. You may lose your appetite or eat constantly. Similarly your sleep habits may change to insomnia, especially waking in the early hours of the morning, or oversleeping. You may feel agitated, restless, or on edge. Your tolerance level is low; everything and everyone gets on your nerves. You feeling fatigued, sluggish, and physically drained. Your whole body may feel heavy, and even small tasks are exhausting. You may suffer from strong feelings of worthlessness or guilt and harshly criticize yourself for just about everything. Trouble concentrating is common so you have trouble focusing, making decisions, or re-membering things. You have unexplained aches and pains, such as headaches, back pain, aching muscles, and stomach pain.

Prozac or other antidepressants are commonly prescribed for depression. Yet, the benefits reported for Prozac by patients are only marginally better than the result reported by patients given placebo drugs, according to studies observed by the FDA. Psychiatrist Tod Mikuriya cited dozens of cases of the successful treatment of clinical depression with marijuana. There is a long history of using pot to get over the blues and the antidepressant effects of marijuana have been confirmed in many human research studies. Medically classified as a euphoriant, marijuana promotes optimistic thinking. While chronic depression may lead to suicide, domestic violence, alcoholism, drug addiction, and other destruc-tive behaviors, there are no similar health risks associated with the mild euphoria or marijuana intoxication.

Best Strains for Depression

There is a debate as to which strain of marijuana has the greatest impact upon depression. Symptoms are individualistic, however, in general Sativa dominant strains tend to be more "up" and Indica dominant strains more relaxing. You will need to experiment.

You can do it empirically—well, sort of. First, stop a couple of times a day and notice how you feel and rate this feeling on a scale of 1 to 9, with 9 being extremely depressed, and 1 being not at all depressed. Record your ratings in a notebook. This is your baseline—a depiction of your "base state" before any intervention. Continue for 3 or 4 days. For fun, you might plot your ratings on a chart.

Now you are ready to experiment. Using your favored method—smoking with a joint or vaporizer, edible, tincture—give yourself a treatment made from Sativa, wait about 10 minutes for inhalation and tinctures and about an hour for edibles, then stop and tune into yourself and rate how you feel using the 1 to 9 scale and record in your notebook. Repeat this process several times, over a period of days, with the Sativa, and then with the Indica. Periodically, take no marijuana and again rate how you feel without this intervention on the 1 to 9 scale.

After a few weeks you should have some very interesting "data". First of all, there should be a substantial decline in your ratings when using the pot. If this is not reflected in your data, then marijuana is probably not an effective treatment for your depression. If the Sativa and Indica strains you used to experiment were pure and distinct, your data should show a differing response to the two strains. Don't get discouraged if you don't see a difference between the two. The experiment is a bit "loose". Try it again for a longer time. Another possibility is that both strains impact your depression in helpful ways.

Setting aside the many nutritional issues with sugar, traditional marijuana edibles are great for depression. Besides the soothing and uplifting effects of the marijuana, sugar promotes serotonin production, which is often under-produced in depressed people. So you get the soothing effect along with the feel-good neurotransmitter.

Dan Danko, author of *High Times Field Guide To Marijuana Strains* analyzed the 16 top strains of medical marijuana. For depressions he recommends Purple Kush, Satori, and Dr. Grinspoons. Purple Kush is almost pure Indica strain that originated in the Pacific Northwest. Its buds are grape-flavored, violet-colored nuggets. Danko says that it can help patients appreciate the deep body stone, which may be helpful in treating chronic pain and depression. Danko says Satori eases depression and anxiety. Dr. Grinspoon, named in honor of the Harvard Medical School marijuana researcher, can be used for the treatment of depression and nausea.

Negative Self-Talk

Your thoughts have a tremendous impact on how you feel—emotionally and physically. If you stop to listen to your thoughts you'll probably notice that they sound like someone talking to you. Sometimes it is a dialog, but usually it's a monologue—an unrelenting harangue of faults, failures and should-haves! This is what psychologists call

Don't believe everything you tell yourself!

"self-talk" because *your thoughts are you talking to yourself.* When depressed you become your own worst enemy, beating yourself up all day long. In most times, you would never talk to others the way you talk to yourself.

We all engage in self-talk. It is part of your thinking process, or what we call "stream of consciousness." As you are presented with problems, or decisions, you might think, "This looks tricky. What should I do first?" or "I better ask for help." or "Oh, this is a piece of cake!"

Self-talk is normal. However, negative self-talk brings you down because all you hear all day long is an exaggerated picture of what a rotten person you are and what a disaster the situation is. It can be paralyzing. You feel down, demoralize, discouraged, dispirited, discouraged. Why? Because you are subjecting yourself to severe self-punishment. You can turn this around, but is difficult because your pessimistic self-talk is self-defeating.

Talk to Yourself Like a Good Friend

If you reduce the negativity of your self-talk, you will probably feel better. The problem is that negativity begets more negativity. One technique is to talk to yourself as a good friend would. When you catch yourself berating yourself, yell, "Stop!" inside your head. Then ask yourself, "What would a good friend say about this?" For example, suppose you make a mistake and catch yourself saying, "You are such an idiot! I can't believe you could do such a dumb thing!" Silently yell, "Stop!" Ask yourself, "What would Joe say about this?" "He'd say, 'Give yourself a break! No one is perfect. You can do better next time." Then say this to yourself. Don't be surprised when the self-criticism sneaks back in. Expect it! Just yell "Stop!" again and switch to talking to yourself like a good friend would.

Learning to talk to yourself like a good friend takes practice. Just keep at it. The more that you catch and stop your punitive self-talk and talk to yourself like a good friend instead, the easier it gets. As you get better at talking to yourself in a friendly way, the better you will feel. You learned to talk to yourself the way that you do, probably from your parents. "You'll never amount to anything!" You have been beating yourself up for decades—and believing all of that bull you've been laying on yourself. It takes effort to change bad habits, especially bad thinking habits. Just keep at it.

Introspection

Marijuana is well known for its ability for promoting introspection. Smoking a few tokes, using a tincture or eating an edible can be a beneficial adjunct to facilitate you talking to yourself like a good friend. One of the things that friends do for friends is to challenge the irrationality of the things you say. Central to psychological "treatment" for negative thinking is to learn to challenge the negative thoughts—just what good friends do!

The introspective tending qualities of pot facilitate this process. The "introspective high" helps to put things into perspective, while simultaneously achieving a kind of distance. Catastrophes become hurtles in your path and disasters become annoyances. Pot sooths anxiety, helping you to calm down. Anxiety doesn't always feel like anxiety, i.e., the jitters. Anxiety can be more veiled, as it drives irrational thinking. Marijuana soothes this away, so that it is easier to talk to yourself like a friend.

Relax and Breathe

Deliberately relax yourself by breathing deeply or by relaxing your muscles, one-by-one. Create your own wonderful vicious cycle. Breathe deeply to relax. Enjoy marijuana's soothing glow, which promotes relaxation of the body—and your mind. Just allow yourself to relax and feel good. Like a good friend, tell yourself that it is okay to feel good. Talk to yourself about other issues like a good friend. A good friend challenges extremes. A good friend is supportive. A good friend is encouraging. A good friend distracts you from unpleasant things. As you relax, it becomes easier to talk to yourself like a good friend. As you talk to yourself in a friendly way, it is easier to relax.

Just have a delicious marijuana treat. Hummm, good. Relax. Breathe deeply, Listen to soothing music and be a good friend to yourself.

Insomnia

SLEEP IS AS IMPORTANT FOR GOOD HEALTH AS DIET and exercise. It restores, rejuvenates and energizes your body and mind. When you sleep, your breathing and heartbeat slow down, your muscles relax, your immunity systems recharge, cells regenerate and repair, and your body conserves energy. Millions of people suffer from insomnia, which has negative effects such as slower reflexes, poor metabolism, slow learning and memory lapse, weight gain, high blood pressure, weakened immune system, dark circles around the eyes, blurred vision, ashy and dull skin. Chronic sleep-loss can cause emotional disturbances, leading to aggressiveness, apathy, and mood swings. Sleep deprivation is used by the military in "enhanced interrogation" so it must be pretty severe!

Sleep affects your ability to do a good job at work. People with insufficient sleep show worse productivity, performance, and safety outcomes on the job. For example, researchers showed that surgeons who worked a night shift and got less than six hours of sleep had more complications in the surgeries they performed, compared to a control group. Other research revealed that sleep-deprived medical residents were more likely to crash their cars and make more mistakes on the job. Sleep-deprived people often don't realize how impaired they are.

Poor sleep can make you fat. People who sleep less are hungrier and consume more calories–perhaps because sleep deprivation leads to hormonal changes that make you crave more carbohydrates and make you feel less like exercising. Lack of sleep can literally kill you. Sleep deprivation might lead to higher blood pressure in seniors. People who sleep fewer than six hours a night are 12% more likely to die prematurely than people who sleep between six and eight hours.

Need for Sleep Changes with Age

As you grow older your need for sleep and your ability to get the sleep you need changes. Your metabolism changes, which means that your energy demands and energy outputs change, and with them, your need for sleep to restore a healthy balance.

The restorative power of sleep is vital for good health. The brain is very active during sleep, especially during REM (rapid eye movement) sleep, when you're dreaming. In all, REM episodes account for about 20–25% of the sleep cycle, or about 2 hours worth in a typical 8-hour stretch.

Melatonin Orchestrates Sleep Pattern

An important aspect of brain activity related to sleep takes place in the pineal gland, a pea-sized object deep within the brain, which produces and secretes the sleep hormone, melatonin (its precursor is the neurotransmitter serotonin), in a cyclic pattern. During the day, bright light entering the eyes sends signals via the optic nerve to the visual cortex, resulting in the sensation of vision. Signals are also sent to a cluster of cells in the anterior hypothalamus called the suprachiasmatic nucleus (SCN), the biological clock that regulates bodily functions that follow the cycle of day and night.

Sleep is one of these cyclic functions. During the day, the SCN signals the pineal gland to inhibit the synthesis of melatonin. When night falls and light stimuli to the SCN diminish, however, the signal is reversed and we become sleepy.

How to Improve Sleep

Physical activity helps sleep. Avoid high protein foods in the evening because they block serotonin production, which aids in sleep. Eating your evening meal early helps to avoid late night digestive challenges. High carbohydrate foods have a mild anti-depressant effect. They also can induce sleep and sometimes reduce pain. So eat a lot of marijuana-laced potatoes, rice, pasta, and bread

Melatonin Plus Marijuana Edibles

Melatonin has long been used as an aid for sleep It's particularly helpful for elderly people with insomnia, who have significantly lower levels of melatonin than age-matched people without insomnia. The amounts used usually range from 0.1 to 5 mg daily; although 2 to 3 mg is typical. Make sure to dim the lights well before bedtime. Harvard's Charles Czeisler cautions that exposure to bright light before bedtime suppresses the melatonin response, and may impair your ability to get to sleep.

The power of the melatonin to promote sleep is enhanced by eating a marijuana edible, such as a "tainted" brownie or cookie about an hour before bedtime. Melatonin is much safer than pharmaceuticals, provided there are no adverse interactions with other drugs you may be taking—your doctor should know.

Bedtime Bud-Milk Cocktail

Sugar in the marijuana brownie or cookie helps sleep because it causes the brain to produce serotonin, the neurotransmitter that plays central role in sleep, moods and brain control. You can promote sleep as well as satisfy your sweet tooth with a glass of orange juice and a marijuana cookie about a half hour before bed.

An alternative is a Bedtime Bud-Milk Cocktail. Warm milk is a well known sleep aid. Heat bud-milk to just below boiling and stir in a teaspoon of sugar or honey. The carbs help get the milk's tryptophan—sleep inducing amino acid—into the brain.

Tryptophan

One of the keys to a restful night's sleep is to get your brain calmed. Some foods contribute to restful sleep; others keep you awake. Sleep-promoting foods contain tryptophan, which is the amino acid that the body uses to make serotonin, the neurotransmitter that slows down nerve traffic so your brain isn't so busy.

Tryptophan is the raw material that the brain uses to build neurotransmitters, serotonin and melatonin. Making more tryptophan available will help to make you sleepy. Eating carbohydrates with tryptophan-containing foods, like mashed potatoes, makes this calming amino acid more available to the brain.

A high carbohydrate meal stimulates the release of insulin, which helps clear amino acids that compete with tryptophan from the bloodstream, allowing more of this natural sleep-inducing amino acid to enter the brain and manufacture sleep-inducing substances, such as serotonin and melatonin. Eating a high-protein meal without accompanying carbohydrates may keep you awake, since protein-rich foods also contain the amino acid, tyrosine, which perks up the brain.

The best bedtime snack is one that has both complex carbohydrates, and perhaps some calcium. Calcium helps the brain use the tryptophan to manufacture melatonin. This explains why dairy products, which contain both tryptophan and calcium, are one of the top sleep-inducing foods. It takes about an hour for tryptophan in food to make it through digestion to the brain, so have your snack about an hour before bedtime.

Lavender

A few drops of lavender essential oil on pillow can soothe anxiety as you sleep.

Best Bedtime Snacks

Foods high in carbohydrates and calcium, and medium-to-low in protein make ideal sleep-inducing bedtime snacks.

Apple pie and ice cream

Whole-grain cereal with milk

Hazelnuts and tofu

Oatmeal and raisin cookies, and a glass of milk

Peanut butter sandwich, ground sesame seeds

Valerian

Valerian has been used for centuries for anxiety and as a sleep aid. From capsules to teas, valerian root is a popular ingredient in many over-the-counter sleep remedies. There is good scientific evidence that it may improve the quality of sleep and reduce the time needed to fall asleep, according to the National Institutes of Health, especially when taken nightly for four to six weeks.

As a sleep aid, valerian seems to be most effective for people who have trouble falling asleep and who consider themselves to be poor sleepers. It also has had good results for people who wake up during the night. People often use valerian in combination with other herbs, including St. John's wort, passionflower, lemon balm, kava, and hops.

Alcohol

Alcohol has paradoxical effects. At first it acts like a sedative but then is converted in the body into a chemical that acts much like a stimulant that awakens you in the middle of the night. You booze, you lose. Alcohol is a depressant, but also activates the sympathetic nervous system in a way that can disrupt sleep. Although wine contains melatonin, it also has the stimulant amino acid tyrosine in it, which can inhibit REM sleep.

Sleep-Enhancing Tips

Cut caffeine consumption in the early afternoon because caffeine can stay in your system for up to eight hours and interrupt falling to sleep. Don't forget that many colas, teas, chocolate, and over-the-counter medicines contain high levels of caffeine—so make sure to read the labels.

Warm feet in a cold room is ideal. The ideal temperature for sleep promotion is between 60 and 68 degrees Fahrenheit. People who sleep well exhibit a drop in core temperature and an increase in dilation in the extremities, so troubled sleepers might try a hot water bottle or bed heater at the feet, while sleeping in a room that's kept in the low 60s.

Cut fat intake. Of fifteen nutrients tracked in a study, fat intake had the highest correlation to poor sleep. Limit liquids in the evening, which can help keep you from having to get up to use the bathroom in the middle of the night. Don't go to bed too hungry or too full. Hunger pangs and indigestion can interrupt sleep.

Relax in the evening. Avoid frightening and highly stimulating movies, like horror films. Meditate and do relaxation exercises. Avoid rigorous exercise in the evening. Listen to soothing music or create "white noise" with a running fan if get traffic noise your bedroom has ambient noise. Hava toke. Eat a marijuana edible.

Keep your bedroom quiet, dark and cool. Have pets sleep in a different room to avoid disturbing you. Don't take naps. Getting too much sleep during the day can make it difficult to fall asleep at night. Get out of bed when you can't sleep. Tossing and turning in bed make you associate insomnia-related frustrations with the bed.

Create a sleep routine. Go to sleep and wake up at the same time every day. A Cornell University sleep expert compared two groups that both got the same amount of sleep. One group went to bed at different times each night, like 11 p.m. one night and 3 am the next; whereas the second group went to sleep at the same time each night. The study showed that the second group was significantly more alert during the day than the erratic sleepers.

Making
Marijuana Medicines

Tinctures

A TINCTURE IS A CONCENTRATED EXTRACT, usually alcohol based. Marijuana tinctures can be made with alcohol, oil or glycerin and are an effective way to use medical marijuana. Drops of the tincture are placed under the tongue—sublingually—where they are rapidly absorbed into the bloodstream. Effects are experienced in 5 to 15 minutes with the peak effect at about 30 minutes after taking the medication. For many patients, the effects are similar to inhaled marijuana.

That no irritating smoke is inhaled is one of the benefits of marijuana tinctures. It is fast-acting and requires no equipment except an eyedropper. Patients who require quick relief of pain, such as for migraine headaches find the tincture's rapid onset very helpful. Patients who are unhappy or uncomfortable with the smoking aspects of marijuana use also enjoy the tinctures because there is no tell-tale smell and it can be used discreetly.

Tinctures were the primary method for delivering cannabis medicine until it was banned in 1937. Tinctures are extractions of whole marijuana—flowers and trim leaves. They are easy to make and very inexpensive. Tinctures contain all 80 of the essential cannabinoids.

Titration, or dose control, is achieved by the number of drops places under the tongue where the medicine is rapidly absorbed into the arterial system and quickly transported to the brain and body. Tinctures can be flavored for better taste.

Don't swallow the tincture because, when swallowed, absorption will be in the GI tract. Instead, place drops under the tongue where they can be absorbed directly into your system. Many patients do, however, like to add the tincture to a cup of tea or cranberry juice for easy delivery. When a tincture is used in a beverage, absorption is slower than if absorbed under the tongue. While tincture absorbed in an empty stomach is accomplished in minutes, conversion in the liver remains, as does the difficulty in titrating dose.

Preparation

There are two major methods of preparing tincture. When selecting a strain, the rule of thumb is to select Indica dominant strains for cramping and muscle spasticity and Sativa dominant strains for pain relief. Often, however, the strain is unknown or not well characterized. Trial and error is generally required to acquire the appropriate strain and the proper dose level.

Alcohol Awareness

Ethanol is the least toxic of all the alcohols. The toxicity of medicines, drugs, and poisons is calibrated by the LD50, meaning the lethal dose for 50 percent, signifying the amount of substance necessary to be fatal. Alcohol is considered in the highly dangerous category. Just five times the amount needed to get you happy can be lethal.

Unlike marijuana, ethanol shares no receptor sites to which it connects. Alcohol intoxication is a true poisoning. Humans possess an enzyme called alcohol dehydrogenase, which helps metabolize ethanol by oxidizing it to acetaldehyde. Other alcohols like methanol, propanol, phenol, and ethylene are extremely poisonous and can cause blindness and even death.

The term *denatured alcohol* means poisonous methanol has been added to prevent drinking, rendering it unsuitable for tinctures ingested orally. When considering dealing with pure grain spirits, it is essential to dilute it with an equal part of water.

It is easy to prepare a tincture from marijuana, that concentrates the active compounds of the plant. You need marijuana (any quality, good or bad, leaves or flowers), ethyl alcohol of 96-99%, a glass jar that can be closed, a coffee filter or a piece of fabric, a deep plate or a frying pan, and a bottle with a dropper.

Marijuana contains many chemicals that can upset the stomach and taste nasty. One of the goals of extraction is to secure the cannabinoids while leaving out as many of the terpenes and chlorophylls as possible. Both heat and light adversely effect cannabinoids and should be avoided or minimized. As the name suggests the cold method does not use heat so keeps the integrity of the cannabinoids intact.

Cold Method

The proof listed on commercial alcohol labels refers to the percentage of ethanol that the beverage contains. The proof is twice the percentage, so "80 proof" means that the mixture contains 40% ethanol. The higher the alcohol content used, the better the extraction will work.

Many folks use Everclear, which is 190 proof or 95% ethanol and has no taste. Unfortunately it is not available in all States. A second favorite is 151 proof rum, which is a light amber 75% ethanol liquid with a sweet taste. Vodka is also popular. These distilled spirits are 40% to 50% ethanol. Some patients find that the higher proofs ethanols burn under the tongue. If burning is a concern substitute a high quality 90-100 proof Vodka.

Everclear and vodka yield a pale green to golden tincture. When 151 rum is used an amber tincture results. Dark green tinctures mean that excess plant material is present so it will taste nasty. Various flavor extracts, like vanilla, raspberry can be added to tinctures made with Everclear. Use only a few drop of flavor extract.

Make sure to use a clean glass—not plastic—jar with a tight lid. One-quart mason jars are ideal. Grind the marijuana thoroughly in a blender until well-ground, but not powdered. Use leaf, bud, shake, joint leftover, or stems. Too many stems will yield a weaker tincture. For higher potency, use shake or bud.

Process

Fill the jar ¾ full of herb; it does not have to be exact. You can use ½ to ¾ part herb. Use the highest proof alcohol available. Pour the alcohol over the marijuana to fill the jar to about an inch or so at the top so that you can shake it. Stir the mixture.

Keep the mixture in a dark and cool place and shake the jar once or twice a day. The alcohol will rise to the top and a deep green/red color will develop. After 2 weeks of aging, strain the tincture through a metal tea strainer or a piece of cloth into a small tincture bottle with a dropper. Leave the rest in the jar to age and mellow for future use.

The marijuana tincture can be used directly, or dissolved in a drink or food, or even vaporized. Use a commercial vaporizer to vaporize your tincture. Alternative you can try the old silver paper system. Form silver paper into a teaspoon like shape and put a few drops of the tincture on it. Carefully heat the tincture with a candle until the alcohol evaporates. Than inhale it using a small tube, like the body of a ball point pen,

Hot Method

Chop the marijuana well. More surface area provides a faster and more efficient extraction. Heat the marijuana. The THC content in the marijuana plant is expressed as THCA (tetrahydrocannabolic acid) prior to decarboxylation into THC, which takes place when marijuana is heated during cooking, when smoked or vaporized. THCA is a mild analgesic and anti-inflammatory but has poor affinity with CB1 receptors. To make a THC-rich tincture that has therapeutic effects similar to when smoked, like including rapid absorption, quick relief and ease of self-titration, the THCA in the plant matter must be converted into THC prior to extracting it through an alcohol soak.

The marijuana must be heated to convert the THCA to THC, but the temperature must stay under 380° F—the temperature at which THC. You can achieve this by spreading the chopped marijuana on a cookie sheet and baking it at 325° F for 3 to 4 minutes.

Always use the highest proof alcohol available. The higher the proof of the alcohol, the more efficient the extraction will be. Simmer the mixture. Heating during extraction drastically decreases extraction times. Use the water bath to heat the alcohol-marijuana mixture to just below the boiling point of ethanol, which is 173° F.

Heating the alcohol mixture can be done safely using a hot water bath. An accurate candy thermometer is needed. Place about 1 inch of water in a 9 x 3 pan. Bring the water to a low simmer. Put the alcohol-marijuana mixture in a one pint mason jar without a lid.

Put the Mason the jar into the simmering water. Then put the thermometer into the jar. Bring the temperature of the mixture to about 165° F. *Do not let boil.* If the mixture starts to bubble, turn

down the water bath. Run the stove hood fan so that alcohol fumes are mixed with water vapor from the water bath and vented out the fan. Your extraction will yield about 1 oz of green dragon tincture. The liquid will be dark green and smell like marijuana.

Storing the Tincture

Always label your tinctures and store in a cool, dark place out of reach of children. Use in dark amber bottles usually available at your local health food store. Keep tinctures away from light and heat. Avoid plastic containers.

Dosage

The dosage varies with the strength of the tincture, size and condition of the person. Strength of the marijuana, ratio of the marijuana to liquid, and length of time in preparation will determine the tincture's strength. Tinctures may be administered directly under the tongue, or diluted in tea, water, or juice. Start with a small dosage, like a half teaspoon, and experiment until you achieve the desired result.

Glycerine-Based Tincture

Marijuana tinctures can be made with vegetable glycerine, instead of alcohol or oil. Always use food grade glycerine. Vegetable glycerine has nearly no impact on blood sugar or insulin and is low in calories. It's sweet taste makes the tincture more palatable than the alcohol-based tinctures.

Grind up 6 ounces of marijuana for 1 gallon of glycerine. Place in a crock pot on low. Never allow mixture to boil. Leave steeping for 24 hours to two days. Test the tincture often to decide when it is done. Alternatively, place the marijuana in a clear, sealed jar in a warm, sunny spot for 4-5 weeks. Some folks leave the mixture in the sun for up to 12 weeks.

Use a cloth and strainer to separate out the marijuana debris from the tincture and it is ready to use.

It takes a lot longer to strain glycerine than it does alcohol. Glycerines have a shorter shelf life than alcohol-based tinctures, so it is best to keep refrigerated. Store in a glass amber bottle for best results.

Compresses and Poultices

A COMPRESS IS A PAD OF ABSORBENT MATERIAL infused with medicine, then pressed onto the painful part of the body to relieve inflammation. A compress can be any temperature—cold, lukewarm, or hot. It can be wet or dry.

When you have pain related to muscle fatigue, a painful carbuncle, or a shiver in your bones, a warm compress can make you feel much better.

Wet Compress

Saturate a washcloth with marijuana oil. Fold the wet cloth and place it in a plastic bag with a zip closure, leaving the bag open. Put in a microwave oven and heat on High for 30-60 seconds. Remove the hot washcloth and bag from microwave carefully, and place on a dry towel. Close the bag. Wrap the towel around the baggie in such a way that it won't slide out and there is a layer of towel between the hot washcloth and your skin.

Place the warm compress over the aching area and leave for about 10 minutes. Remove and allow the area to cool. Reheat the washcloth and repeat.

Poultices

A poultice is a soft, mushy preparation composed of a pulpy or mealy herbal substance that can absorb a large amount of fluid.

The herbal matter is mashed into a paste using hot liquids and spread thickly on a cloth and applied, while hot, to the painful or inflamed area if the body. Poultices work through moist heat, which must be renewed after several minutes or otherwise kept warm. The cloth can then be covered with plastic wrap to hold in the moisture. The poultice should be changed whenever it dries out.

A poultice can be used to draw out infection, treat boils and abscesses, relieve inflammation or a rash or simply draw the poison from a bee sting!

Some patients soak marijuana leaves in alcohol and apply them as a poultice to an arthritic

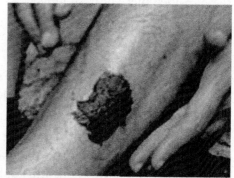

Poultice drawing out a boil.

or swollen joint. Poultices can be used to heal bruises, break up congestion, reduce inflammation, withdraw pus from putrid sores, soothe abrasions, or withdraw toxins from an area. They may be applied hot or cold, depending on the health need. Cold poultices are used to withdraw the heat from an inflamed or congested area. Use a hot poultice to relax spasms and for some pains.

A compress is used the same way but usually warm liquids are applied to the cloth instead of raw substances. Tinctures or herbal infusions are great for compresses.

How to Make a Poultice

If you are using fresh herbs, mix half a cup of the herbs with one cup of water in a saucepan and simmer it for two minutes. With dried herbs, simply mix together the herbs and warm water to make a paste. Pour the mixture onto a piece of cloth and apply it to the affected area. Then secure the gauze or cloth with a bandage or towel.

Marijuana-Ginger Poultice

Ingredients:

3-inch piece of fresh ginger

1/4 cup bud-oil

PEEL AND FINELY MINCE THE GINGER and mix with bud-oil to form a paste. Apply to the painful joint. You may want to wrap the marijuana-ginger poultice in place with an ace bandage. Leave in place for 10-15 minutes. For extra relief warm the marijuana-ginger for 15 seconds in microwave before applying.

Marijuana-Chamomile Tea Poultice

Ingredients:

4 chamomile tea bags

2 tbsp bud-oil

BREW A STRONG INFUSION using four chamomile tea bags in a cup of hot water. Cover and steep for 20 minutes, then squeeze and remove tea bags. Add bud-oil and mix well. Soak a clean cloth in the liquid and apply to aching joint or muscle.

Marijuana-Mustard Poultice

Bronchitis, asthma and pneumonia can be treated by applying a marijuana-mustard poultice on the chest area. It is maintained as long as the burning sensation is not strong, it is then removed and the area is to be covered with a warm material. Asthma can be treated by applying marijuana-mustard poultice to chest for 20 minutes.

Marijuana-Mustard Poultice

Ingredients

　¼ cup mustard flour

　¼ cup marijuana, powdered

　Water

MIX MUSTARD, MARIJUANA WITH WARM MUSTARD until a soft paste is formed. Put the paste between two cloths and applied to the troublesome area for about 15 to 30 minutes.

Marijuana Liniment

A LINIMENT IS AN EXTERNAL APPLICATION that is rubbed into the skin. There are two methods to make liniments. The first method is the same as used for making tinctures with alcohol only you use rubbing alcohol, which is toxic if taken internally. Be sure to label your liniment: "For External Use Only."

In the second method, boil the marijuana root in water until you have a concentrated mixture, then add rubbing alcohol. This is an age-old folk remedy for relief of arthritis and sore muscle pain.

Topical Marijuana Liniment

Ingredients

3-7 g. marijuana leaf, ground fine

Rubbing alcohol

G RIND MARIJUANA INTO A FINE POWDER. Pour about 1/3 bottle of rubbing alcohol into a separate container for future use. Using a funnel, pour the ground marijuana into the bottle. Shake well, then store in a dark place. Shake daily, for 1-2 months. Using a cloth strain out solid material. Apply liberally to affected area for pain relief, as needed. Good for arthritis, and muscle pain.

Salves and Balms

SALVE IS A BROAD TERM used to describe lotions, ointments, pastes, and creams that soothe or heal an area of the body that is excessively dry, irritated, burned, or wounded. In many cases, salves contain natural ingredients that can promote the healing process and reduce discomfort in the area being treated. They are commonly used to treat severely dry hands, chapped lips, and sunburned skin. Marijuana salves have been used to relieve muscle aches and pains for generations. They relieve topical pain and can be used in combination with other herbs. Salves can be messy, however.

Prepare a salve by using coconut oil and marijuana and cooking in the same fashion as when making bud-butter. Adding other medicinal plants like aloe, comfrey, yarrow, ginger can greatly help with the healing qualities. The more plant material the better. Cool overnight. Then separate the oil from the water. Heat the oil again to boil off any additional water and pour into a glass jar.

Apply the salve to area with pain, spasm, or damage. Use a nice amount but don't try to over-saturate area. For best results, apply after a hot shower.

Medicated Marijuana Salve

Ingredients:

4 cups olive oil

1 cup St. Johns wort

2 cups dried calendula blossoms

1/4 cup comfrey root

1/4 cup lavender flowers

6 tbsp coconut oil

1 1/2 cups dried marijuana leaf

2 -3 tbsp beeswax

HEAT THE OILS AND ADD THE DRIED ROOTS and keep just below the simmer point. If you see bubbles then turn down. Steep the herbs for 2 to 3 hours, stirring every once in awhile. Cool and strain using a cloth. Place in a clean bowl and add beeswax.

Other oils, like hemp oil, can be substituted or added along with various medicinal dried herbs and plant oils. The salve is great for bug bites, stings and scratches.

Quick Headache Salve

Ingredients:

Coco Butter

Tincture marijuana

Lavender essential oil

FILL A SHOT GLASS HALF FULL of coco butter, add the marijuana tincture and lavender oil. Stir and apply to temples.

Hemp Salve

One of the most powerful hemp preparations is the hemp salve. Its efficiency was proven already in the 50s at the Olomouc University Hospital, where Prof. Jan Kabelik carried out his famous research on the antibacterial effects of Cannabis Indica.

One of the hospital pathologists cut his finger during an autopsy. Bacteria resistant to antibiotics infected the wound. Someone ask Prof. Kabelik for help because of his research on the medical use of cannabis. Hemp salve was applied to the infected wound and two days later the wound was healing. Amputation was avoided.

Vaseline is a good salve base for people suffering from allergies, although it does not penetrate as well as other bases.

The hemp salve is a universal healing preparation with multiple effects, combining the effects of an antibiotic ointment with the soothing effects of a salve to efficiently relieve arthritic and rheumatism pains. It is very efficient for the treatment of burns, certain eczemas, psoriasis and fungus. New use the salve on bleeding wounds.

Hemp Salve

Ingredients:

1 jar Vaseline

100 g. marijuana leaves, crushed or

50 g. marijuana buds, crushed

MELT HALF OF THE VASELINE IN A LARGE POT, add marijuana and cook slowly for 20 minutes. Cool mixture. Add 4 gallons water, bring to the boiling point, and slowly cook for 2 hours. Cool and refrigerate overnight. Take out the fatty cake and press to eliminate the water. Spread the cake on a cookie sheet, cover it and let it ferment for 3 weeks in a dark place at room temperature.

Put the mixture into a large pot and add the second half of Vaseline and melt it. Slowly cook the mixture until the fermentation smell dissipates. Strain through a strainer and pour the resulting green liquid into the top of a double boiler with water in the lower pan. Add finely crushed buds and cook in the water bath for an hour, stirring frequently. A light skim will form on the surface. Cool the mixture and store in a cool, dark place for a week to 10 days. Cook again in the top of a double boiler in water. Store the mixture in a dark, cool place for a week or so.

Again melt and cook the mixture as in the top of the double boiler. Strain through a strainer and then through a cloth. Pour the salve into small cosmetic jars.

Arthritis Balm

Ingredients

4 oz marijuana leaf

Water

1 1/4 cup hemp oil

1-2 oz beeswax

PUT MARIJUANA IN A LARGE STOCK POT, cover with water and add hemp oil. Bring to a boil and simmer at a low boil for 5-6 hours, adding water as needed. Allow to cool and strain through cloth, saving the liquid. Place the liquid into the refrigerator over night. Peel the hemp oil layer off the top and place into a small pot and melt over low heat. Add beeswax, mix well, and cool into a salve.

Cannabis-Castor Oil Pack

MIX BUD-OIL AND CASTOR OIL for a pack to fight inflammation, to help Carpal Tunnel Syndrome or to soothe a strain. Apply the cannabis-caster oil to a cloth and place it on the injured area, like your wrist. Cover the area with plastic wrap. Place another rag on top of the plastic wrap and apply a heating pad for 30-45 minutes. The cannabis-castor oil is absorbed through the skin and help to reduce the inflammation in a very powerful way.

Healing Oils

FRAGRANCE AND HEALING CHEMICALS from the medicinal plants, including marijuana, can be infused into essential oils, also called infused oils, which can be inhaled for health benefit. When inhaled, the oil's essences passes directly from the lungs into the blood stream where they are quickly carried to the brain's nerve centers.

What Are Infused Oils?

An infused oil consists of a carrier oil that has been permeated or infused with one or more herbs and contains the therapeutic properties of both the carrier oil and the herbs that were infused into the oil. It is best to make only small quantities because oils go rancid pretty quickly. To extend its life, keep refrigerated.

Infused oils are not used for cooking and don't come from seeds or nuts. Infused oils are highly concentrated distillation of leaves and flowers of the herb itself. They capture the plants chemical compounds and vaporize easily.

How to Make Infused Bud-Oil

A easy way to make an infused oil is with a crock pot on a very low heat setting. The infused oil must be gently heated, so it is essential that you do not overheat the oil.

Add 2 ounces of carrier oil and 1/2 - 2/3 ounce of dried marijuana buds to the crock pot and stir well. Heat on the lowest setting for two hours, stirring every 10-15 minutes. Strain the oil through a cloth or coffee filter twice.

Healing Infused Oils

Infused oils made from lavender, marjoram, and sandalwood can alter brain waves when breathed, helping to induce relaxation and sleep. Infused oils are used to relieve anxiety and depression, soothe stress, aid sleep, and build energy. Rubbing essential oils into the skin or inhaling steam of essential oils can ease pain, relieve congestion, and treat infections.

Herb	Healing Benefits
Basil	Antiseptic, eases muscle spasms, calms nerves. Use for headaches, bronchitis, colds, coughs.
Chamomile	Relieves pain, antidepressant, anti-inflammatory, sedative. Use for stress, arthritis, bursitis.
Eucalyptus	Pain reliever, decongestant, antiviral, antibacterial, antifungal. Use for asthma, coughs, bronchitis, arthritis, headache.
Geranium	Pain reliever, antidepressant, anti-inflammatory. Use for stress, anxiety.
Lavender	Antidepressant, sedative, relieves muscle spasms. Good for arthritis, pain, stress, anxiety, insomnia
Lemon	Eases muscle spasms, antibacterial, antifungal depression, fatigue.
Peppermint	Pain reliever, relieve muscle spasms, pain, decongestant. Use for headache, colds, nausea, muscle spasms, lethargy, depression.
Rosemary	Pain reliever, antiseptic, eases muscle spasms, decongestant, stimulant. Use for fatigue, asthma,, bronchitis, cramps, muscle soreness, arthritis, headache, stress, depression.
Tea Tree	Antibiotic, antibacterial, antiviral, decongestant. Use for cuts, insect bites, colds, bronchitis
Thyme	Pain reliever, antibacterial. Use for arthritis, colds.

Marijuana-Mint Pain Relief Oil

MINT RUBBED ON THE FOREHEAD and temples of chronic headache sufferers eased their pain. Mint is an ingredient in many traditional saves and oils for soothing aching muscles.

Ingredients:

 2 cups fresh mint leaves

 ¼-1/2 cup bud-oil

Loosely fill a small clean jar with the fresh mint leaves. Cover mint leaves with oil mixture to fill jar. Allow mixture to sit on a sunny window and steep for at least 2 weeks. Then strain it and transfer solution into a clean jar or small bottle. Store in a cool dark place. Rub into aching joints as needed.

Spicy Marijuana Massage Oil

Ingredients:

 1 tbsp dried rosemary leaves

 3 tsp celery seeds

 2 tsp crushed cayenne

 1/2 cup bud-oil

MIX ROSEMARY, CELERY SEEDS, CAYENNE and pulverized in a clean coffee grinder. Spoon into glass jar with tight-fitting lid and add oil. Shake vigorously, then cover and leave for 10 days, shaking daily. Strain through a coffee filter into a glass bottle and keep in a cool, dark place for up to 6 months, longer if refrigerated. Gently massage a little of the oil onto the aching joint twice a day to relieve pain and inflammation.

Marijuana Capsules

Capsules are an easy, convenient way to take medical marijuana. As you gain experience in preparation you can standardize your dosages—at least for each batch, which can be many dozen capsules.

Empty capsules are available at pharmacies and health food stores. Get a size convenient for you to swallow. If you are unable to obtain capsules, an alternative is to simply purchase some inexpensive herbal capsules and empty out the contents.

Quick Method

Make a paste of 1 gram ground marijuana, one drop of liquid lecithin, and just enough hemp- or bud-oil to make the paste on the dry side. Stuff the bottom part of the capsule with the paste. Put the capsule together and store in a cool, dry place until ready to use. One gram of marijuana should make four capsules.

Stove Top Method

Clean the buds by removing all seeds and sticks. Chop buds into powder using a blender. Let the powder settle before opening lid so it doesn't fly out. Pour powdered marijuana into double boiler. Using a spatula, sweep the powder that clings to the glass, lid and blades into the top pan of the double boiler.

Fill the bottom of the double boiler partially with water and set on the stove to boil. While the bottom pan is heating, mix the oil into the herb in the top pan of the double boiler using the spatula. When done mixing, the powder will look much darker and barely sticking together.

Place the top pan into the top of the double boiler. Put the cooking thermometer into center of the mixture. Watch closely so that sure the mixture does not go above 275 degrees Fahrenheit because THC vaporizes at around 300 F. Stir the herb mixture continuously while heating, as soon as the herb hits 250 degrees, lower the temperature and maintain around 250 degrees for 10 minutes cooking time. Avoid overheating the mixture or you will vaporize some of the THC and lose medicinal value.

Remove the top pan from the double boiler and put it into a sink of cool water, stirring the mixture to hasten cooling. When cool to the touch, place the top pan into the freezer to chill. Scrape mixture out of the pan and chop into powder. Pack the empty gelatin capsules with the powder.

When all the capsules are filled, place them into an airtight pill bottle and store it in the freezer.

Microwave Method

Place the marijuana powder in a microwave safe bowl and cover the top with 3-4 layers of plastic wrap. Microwave the bowl for 10 to 15 seconds repeatedly. If the plastic wrap bulges upwards, stop cooking and wait for the bulge to go down, then zap it again. Repeat this cycling process for 5 minutes, then place the still-sealed bowl into the freezer and leave until chilled to keep the THC vapors contained. Chop the cooled mixture into a powder and fill capsules.

Index

Ronin Books for Independent Minds

GROWING MARIJUANA HYDROPONICALLY.. Hans GROHYD 16.95 ___
Sea-of-green,cottage approach, perpetual harvest, nutrients, lights.

THE HEALING MAGIC OF CANNABIS .... Potter/Joy HEAMAG 14.95 ___
Healing power of psychoactivity, tinctures, food, list of med conditions.

MARIJUANA FOOD HANDBOOK .... Drake MARFOO 14.95 ___
Impressive range of options for cooking with cannabis..

MARIJUANA LAW, 2ND EDITION .... Boire MARLAW 17.95 ___
Increase privacy protections and reduce exposure to arrest.

CANNABIS ALCHEMY .... Gold CANALC 16.95 ___
Classic and modern techniques to enhance potency.

GROWING EXTRAORDINARY MJ .... Gottlieb GROEXT 12.95 ___
Sea of green, perpetually harvest techniques, nutrients, lights

LEGAL HIGHS .... Gottlieb LEGHIG 12.95 ___
An encyclopedia of relatively unknown legal psychoactive herbs & chemicals.

POLITICS OF ECSTASY .... Leary POLECS 14.95 ___
Tim Leary's classic essays on the pursecution of enjoying ecstatic states.

COOKING WITH CANNABIS .... Gottlieb COOCAN 12.95 ___
The "classic" marijuana cookbook from the 1970s!.

MARIJUANA BOTANY .... Clarke MARBOT 24.95 ___
Sexing, cultivation, THC production and peak potency, continued production.

MEDICAL MARIJUANA LAW .... Boire/Feeney MEDLAW 16.95 ___
Pratical, tactical manual for patients, caretakers, providers, doctors.

CULTIVATOR'S HANDBOOK OF MARIJ .... Drake CULMAR 24.95 ___
Land and light concerns, harvesting and curing, psycoactive tobacco

THE FUGITIVE PHILOSOPHER .... Leary FUGPHI 12.95 ___
Leary's incredible sage and philosophy.

PASS THE TEST .... Potter/Orfali PASTES 16.95 ___
How tests work, how to beat test, what to do if tested positive.

SACRED MUSHROOMS & THE LAW .... Boire SACMUS 12.95 ___
Cognitive liberty, review of Federal & State laws & possible defenses.

PEYOTE & OTHER PSYCHOACTIVE CACTI .... Gottlieb PEYOTE 12.95 ___
Cultivation, grafting, cloning, nutrients, extractions, glossary of alkaloids, suppliers.

PROGRAMMIN THE HUMAN BIOCOMPUTER .. Lilly PROHUM 12.95 ___
Manual on self-metaprogramming with entheogens..

Books prices: **SUBTOTAL** $_____

CALIF customers add sales tax 9.75% $_____

BASIC SHIPPING: (All orders) **$6.00**

Make sure to add in the per book shipping fee - essential!

+ **SHIPPING**: add USA+$1/bk, Canada+$2/bk, Europe+$7/bk, Pacific+$10/bk $_____

Books + Tax + Basic + Shipping: TOTAL $_____

Checks payable to **Ronin Publishing**

MC _ Visa _ Exp date __ - __ card #: _

Phone # (Req for CC orders)_ _ _ _ _ _ _ _ _ _ _ _ _ _ Signature_ _ _ _ _ _ _ _ _ _ _ _ _ _

Name_ _

Address _ _ _ _ _ _ _ _ _ _ _ _ _ _ City _ _ _ _ _ _ _ _ _ _ _ State _ _ _ ZIP _ _ _ _ _

Ronin Publishing, Inc.
Box 22900, Oakland, CA 94609• Ph: 800/858-2665 • Fax: 510/420-3672
ronin@roninpub.com • www.roninpub.com - Catalog online
Visit our site • Call for free catalog • Wholesale queries welcome